Celebrating

THE *Seasons*

at Westerbeke Ranch

Celebrating THE *Seasons*

at Westerbeke Ranch

John Littlewood

Celebrating the Seasons at Westerbeke Ranch

Published by Happy Palate Press
P. O. Box 430, Sonoma, CA 95476
www.hppress.com

First edition printed 2005
10 9 8 7 6 5 4 3 2 1

Publisher's Cataloging-in-Publication Data
Littlewood, John W., 1960–
Celebrating the Seasons at Westerbeke Ranch/by John Littlewood—1st ed.

Library of Congress Control Number 2005921913

Includes indexes.
1. Cookery   I. Littlewood, John W.   II. Title
ISBN 0-9761136-051995

Printed on acid-free paper
Printed in the United States of America

Cover design by Steve Graydon with Jill Hunting
Page design by Steve Graydon and Jill Hunting
Front cover dessert photograph and back cover portrait by Robert Herzog
All other photographs taken at Westerbeke Ranch by John Littlewood
Photograph on page 98 by John Littlewood, taken at and published with permission
of Sonoma Valley Museum of Art
Excerpt of poem on page 105 published with permission of California Poets in the
Schools

For Rudy

Contents

Contents continued

Contents

Contents continued

• *Recipe is suitable for vegan diets*

Foreword

In 1935, Richard and Muriel Van Hoosear, owners of a prospering grain and seed business in San Francisco, purchased ninety acres at the foot of Sonoma Mountain, in the "Valley of the Moon." They wanted a place where their three daughters—Patricia, Marilyn, and Joyce—could run around and scrape their knees. For thirty years "the Ranch" in Sonoma provided a rustic retreat for the Van Hoosear family. Much of the grounds of the Westerbeke Ranch and Conference Center were developed during those early years.

By the late 1960s, Patricia and her husband Don Westerbeke, my parents, were envisioning the Ranch as more than a family retreat. What began as a penchant for hosting fabulous family celebrations and successful fund-raisers for schools and charities grew into a desire to foster and participate in the social-consciousness movement that was brewing in the '60s and '70s. Many of the movement's bright lights passed through the San Francisco Bay Area, and Patricia and Don always seemed to be somewhere near the center of the action.

At first my parents invited people to come to the Ranch to relax. Writers, thinkers, and activists from around the world—including Joseph Campbell, Dolores Krieger, Carl Rogers, Elisabeth Kübler-Ross, and Werner Erhard—were frequent weekend guests. They sprawled around the pool under the summer sun and enjoyed sumptuous meals cooked by Patricia and her crew. Rustic cabins made up with fresh linens awaited tired guests after late-night conversations around the communal table or in the waning glow of a fire. The conversations were wide-ranging and often profound.

Eventually, a bit of order was imposed on this freewheeling "salon" of intellectual ferment and indulgent relaxation. The Ranch began hosting workshops organized around ideas or themes. Inspired by Don Westerbeke's miraculous healing in the early 1970s, by a doctor in the Philippines who cured him of a brain tumor, Patricia and Don decided to build the Ranch into a center for alternative healing and spiritual/psychological growth. Underlying their idea was a hope that the Ranch could become a business, to help keep clean sheets on the beds and bountiful meals on the table. Happily, Don and Patricia's vision of the Ranch as a thriving business has born fruit, while guests continue to enjoy a tranquil and caring environment—the kind of environment we believe is most conducive to personal growth.

Over the years at Westerbeke Ranch, food has always been the central pleasure. From Patricia's experiments with international cuisines in the '60s to the sophistication of today's fresh fusion cooking, the ranch kitchen has been as much a place of innovation and bold ideas as the workshops going on around it. The serenity and natural beauty of the setting, the simple rustic charm of the cabins and old adobe, and the warm, personal touch of the family and staff have always made the Ranch unique. Still, food has been the thread that draws our guests together, binding them in that most ancient and sacred of rituals, breaking bread. Truly, the kitchen is the heart of the Ranch.

Mealtimes are announced by the clanging of a great iron triangle, which can be heard across the Ranch and probably into the next county. Guests gather boisterously at the buffet or around the massive redwood table, while from behind two battered swinging doors, piquant aromas waft from the kitchen into the dining room. Hungry anticipation builds. The banter of the kitchen staff rises and falls as they bend to the task at hand, until at last the doors swing open and the meal is set out, buffet-style. Then the chef explains the meal and tells us which local farm the vegetables came from or what inspired his recipes. It is not uncommon for the guests to spontaneously applaud the kitchen staff when they come out with the dessert course.

Westerbeke Ranch has tested the mettle of many excellent cooks. The task of trying to please a wide variety of guests is never easy. Keeping up the spirits and focus of the kitchen staff, while making the menu fresh and interesting, requires discipline and personal skills not often found among gifted, creative people. Yet John Littlewood, our executive chef, is one of those rare individuals who combine great artistry with a compassionate and generous spirit. The recipes he has chosen for this book have all been rigorously (and enthusiastically) evaluated by legions of Ranch guests and staff. With John as your guide, now you can enjoy the "flavor" of Westerbeke Ranch and bring to your own table the warmth and savory delight we have come to know and appreciate through his art.

Wendy Westerbeke

Introduction

Celebrating the Seasons is an invitation to join me in the kitchen of Westerbeke Ranch. It is also, in a sense, the story of my culinary journey, because the recipes are all based on a cooking style I've been developing for more than twenty years. First, let me welcome you to this peaceful place and tell you a little about myself.

Westerbeke Ranch is just a few miles from the town of Sonoma, California, about an hour's drive north of San Francisco. Famous for its wines, Sonoma Valley reminds me of the south of France: it has a thriving food culture, a Mediterranean climate, and a soft light that brushes the hills with changing colors throughout the day.

Arriving at the Ranch, you walk through an arched gate covered with orange trumpet vine. Next you see an exuberant herb and flower garden that, depending on the season, is full of roses, lavender, poppies, and nasturtiums, along with a few fruit trees. A burbling, urn-shaped birdbath and benches invite you to pause before you climb the steps to a large deck. On the right are a large swimming pool, several umbrella-shaded tables, and the terra cotta–roofed building we call "the Adobe." A Mexican-tile floor keeps the dining area cool in summer, and two great fireplaces keep it toasty in winter. In this comfortable setting I present a kind of culinary theater three times a day. "Backstage," just beyond the swinging doors, is the area where I spend many of my waking hours cooking, experimenting with new recipes, and recording them.

My kitchen career began near Carmel, California, washing dishes in a vegetarian restaurant. I was seventeen and eager to learn, so it wasn't long before I moved to the pantry, where salads and desserts were "plated." Soon I was working at an elegant French restaurant and tasting rich, classic sauces such as Mornay and demi-glace for the first time. Little did I know how much these flavors would linger in my memory and influence the course of my life.

A few years later I moved to Marin County in the San Francisco Bay Area, where I found a job as a prep cook in a soup and salad restaurant. Even in this casual, inexpensive restaurant, my passion for cooking was growing. As a college student in Boulder, Colorado, I took a job in a lively seafood restaurant and worked my way up to head grillman, then moved to the catering department of a large, historic hotel with three separate restaurants. Working with different chefs and catering weddings, casual outdoor barbecues, and elegant parties in penthouses whetted my appetite for more. I graduated with a degree in journalism, but more important was what I had learned about food and wine, and where I wanted to go.

I enrolled at the California Culinary Academy in San Francisco. The scope of choices presented there showed me that the culinary arts could provide a lifetime of challenges and rewards. *Garde manger* ("in charge of food") class taught me how to make complex terrines and pâtés, and how to poach whole salmon and decorate them with "scales" made from cucumber slices. Wine courses ushered me into the exciting alchemy of the grape. I found pastry work—a fascinating blend of science, art, and craft—especially exciting. Other classes hammered home the importance of timing, technique, and organization. A seminar on taste focused on pairing food and wine. I waited tables for the first time and made some embarrassing mistakes (for example, spilling wine on one of my instructors and his wife), gaining new respect for well-trained servers.

During my last semester at the Culinary Academy, I began to dream of cooking in France, and with the help of friends I was in Lyon within a year of graduation. At the Michelin-starred restaurant Larivoire, near the Rhône River, I practiced the techniques of classic cuisine. Kitchen hierarchy in France is based on the "brigade" system of various stations for vegetables and side dishes, entrées, fish, and pastry. As an apprentice I rotated through the kitchen, spending a few weeks in each station.

Again, it was pastry that drew me in. The pâtisserie seemed calm and orderly compared to the hectic hot kitchen. Perfect fresh fruit for tarts, cakes, and sauces arrived daily, and top-notch French chocolate came from a town nearby. I enjoyed the precision of pastry work—so different from savory cooking, where recipes are the exception, not the rule. My education continued after hours, as the other cooks and I prepared and enjoyed multicourse dinners, always paired with excellent wines.

Next came Paris. Exploring the Left Bank, I discovered a cookbook store crammed with every imaginable book about food and wine. The charming, gregarious owner quickly found me a job at an elegant restaurant near the Champs Elysées. The chefs at Ivan cooked a modern cuisine, very different from the lyonnaise style, experimenting with nontraditional ingredients including coriander and star anise, and creating unusual combinations such as rosemary with caramel. When the pastry chef went on vacation, it was my job to greet the delivery trucks at six A.M., gather up the paper bags stuffed with long, fragrant baguettes, and unlock the door. I'd make myself an espresso and start the day's work: baking hundreds of delicate wafer cookies and tangy lemon tartlets, rolling buttery chocolate ganache in cocoa powder to make truffles, and preparing trembly grapefruit terrines and rich, white nougat ice cream.

It wasn't long before I was offered the job of sous chef in a luxury hotel in St. Croix, Virgin Islands. After training with European chefs (mostly male and often short-tempered), working with a friendly, creative female chef was a welcome change.

We approached island cuisine as a team. Creamy coconut milk, spiny lobster, the abalone-like conch, and the impossibly hot habanero chile were all part of my introduction to tropical cooking. However, after a year on the island I was eager to return to California.

Once again in San Francisco, I partnered up with an innovative designer to re-open what had been a run-down restaurant. Unfortunately, it turned out to be one of the scores that close there each year. Luckily, a new opportunity quickly presented itself. For several years I was executive chef and cooking instructor at a historic hotel in the Sierra Foothills. Simultaneously running a fine dining establishment and teaching was at once exhausting and exhilarating. I gleaned two valuable "nuggets" in the gold country: good teachers are lifelong students, and patience truly is a virtue. After five years I sought new inspiration. It was time for another trip to Europe.

Armed with a three-month visa, my résumé, and a few good knives, I flew to London. Wandering around the Portobello market one warm afternoon, I strolled into a store called Books for Cooks. A terse advertisement tacked to the wall read "Chef wanted, luxury hotel barge in Burgundy, France." The flyer attracted me like a trained dog to truffles, and a week later I found myself on Le Papillon, a beautifully restored, hundred-year-old barge docked on the Yonne River in Auxerre, near Chablis. The imposing thirteenth-century Saint Etienne cathedral, with its tall stained-glass windows and flying buttresses, stood watch over the boats on the quay.

In the long, narrow kitchen amidships, two arched windows allowed me an ever-changing vista as we slowly made our way up and down the river via the ancient system of locks. One minute I'd be looking at a wet stone wall as the barge was lifted by water rushing through the old gates, then the scene would gradually change to a smiling lock-tender, whose curious dog eagerly sniffed the aromas wafting from my galley. Changing menus paid tribute to France and to Burgundy in particular, such as braised rabbit with Dijon mustard sauce, escargot in crêpes with garlic-parsley-butter sauce and red wine essence, roasted breast of duck with cassis sauce and haricots verts, and apple tarte Tatin.

Between trips I rented a car and toured the region of Champagne, visiting the historic chalk wine caves of Veuve Clicquot, Moët & Chandon, and Pommery. Another trip took me to Mâcon, where I enjoyed the celebrated white wines of the area. I've never forgotten the greenish-gold, wildly floral, matchless Pouilly-Fuissé that was a lesson in itself about flavors in perfect balance.

This immersion in French food and wine, combined with my quest for new culinary experiences and a longstanding love for northern California, pointed me to Sonoma.

After a few years of catering wine country events, however, I wondered if I had chosen wisely. Then I found the Ranch. With its natural beauty, emphasis on personal growth, and opportunity for creative expression, I felt I had come home. The Westerbeke family and staff greeted me as if I had only been away for a while, though we had never met.

When the kitchen crew assembled for our first staff meeting, I was greeted with curious faces awaiting instructions. I stated my simple philosophy: to please everyone with delicious, beautiful food, to foster personal growth, and to make work fun. These "rules" guide our day-to-day operations, and I think you will find they have shaped this book.

Since arriving at the Ranch, I have adapted to our guests' preferences for a light, contemporary cuisine. Sautéeing and frying usually give way to roasting and grilling. Olive oil and coconut milk stand in for butter and cream. Yogurt often replaces mayonnaise, and chutney might fill in for a meat-based brown sauce. California's multiculturalism and my travels are reflected in our menus. Latin and Asian flavors lead the way, and dishes inspired by the cuisines of France, Italy, and the Mediterranean appear on a regular basis. Vegetarian choices are always available. Lunch might be chicken mole, chayote with jalapeño and lime, and roasted vegetables with poblano purée. For dinner, I might serve roasted halibut with coconut-tomato-basil sauce, basmati rice, and fresh mangoes with crystallized-ginger ice cream.

Although seasonality is the theme I've used to organize this book, my recipes rarely depend on an ingredient that is available in just one season. I often suggest substitutions. For example, the **Orange-lime curd** recipe can just as easily be made with Meyer lemons in wintertime. Recipes are not written in stone. If you don't have fresh fruit, try frozen. If salmon isn't available, try halibut. Stay flexible.

With simplicity in mind, I've forsaken complicated techniques in favor of cooking methods that save time without sacrificing flavor. Throughout *Celebrating the Seasons* you'll find delicious dishes that go together quickly, such as **Pork chile verde, Tofu with hot-sweet sauce,** and **Chayote putanesca.** More difficult recipes will inspire budding cooks, like my friend who tried the Ciabatta recipe, having never made bread, and turned out two beautiful loaves.

Cooking and sharing food are some of life's greatest pleasures. Like the dishes from my kitchen, this book has been prepared with pride. It gives me immense joy to present it to you.

Using This Book

Celebrating the Seasons is designed so that you can find a menu you like and then cook it. But there are other ways to use this book:

- Look through it for information, ideas, and tips.
- Browse the contents pages, menus, or indexes for a single dish that sounds good to you. The occasion doesn't have to be a holiday; many dishes are year-round people-pleasers.
- Go to the indexes and search by degree of difficulty, or browse by recipe name or ingredient.
  - Pick and choose recipes from different chapters to create your own menu.

Words in SMALL CAPITAL LETTERS are defined in the glossary, which you'll find in the Resources section. Recipe names that are cross-referenced and/or listed in the indexes look like this example: **Green rice**.

Always read a recipe from beginning to end before you start cooking. This helps in numerous ways, such as:

- Creating a shopping list: What am I going to need?
- Getting organized: What do I need first? Then what happens? What kind of equipment am I going to need?
- Understanding what the finished dish will be like.
- Getting an overall idea of the time and energy involved. For example, the requirements for **Orange-lime curd** are much different than for **Chicken mole poblano**.

Many cookbooks recommend measuring all ingredients before starting a recipe. It's good advice, and especially important when:

- The recipe involves a fast technique such as wok cookery and it is essential to have all ingredients ready to go.
- The recipe is complex and/or it's your first time making it.
- It's a pastry recipe. These usually require more precision than savory recipes.

Most of my recipes include notes. These might be shortcuts, possible substitutions for certain ingredients, or variations to try. I like recipes that are versatile and interchangeable, and I'll show you how to use leftovers creatively and make the most of your time in the kitchen.

Seasonal Menus
and Recipes

Spring Menus

Earth Day Buffet

Easter Brunch

Cinco de Mayo Fiesta

Memorial Day Picnic

Earth Day Buffet

Earth Day focuses our attention on making responsible choices for the environment and fostering harmony among those with whom we share the planet. Sharing a meal always creates a sense of community. So let's gather round, break bread, and honor Mother Earth.

MARCH 20 OR 21, OR APRIL 22 (DATE VARIES)

Sautéed chicken breasts
with browned-garlic butter sauce

Buttermilk mashed potatoes

Green beans with
easy miso sauce

Green salad with candied pecans
and pear-sherry dressing

Poppy seed angel food cake
with orange-lime curd

Sautéed chicken breasts
with browned-garlic butter sauce

This recipe produces flavorful, juicy chicken. Browned garlic gives the sauce a wonderful toasty flavor, and the butter makes it silky smooth.

Serves 6

Browned-garlic butter sauce (recipe follows)
6 boneless skinless chicken breast halves
Kosher salt
Black pepper
¾ cup all-purpose flour
¼ cup canola oil
½ cup dry white wine or water

1. Make **Browned-garlic butter sauce.**
2. Sprinkle chicken breasts lightly with salt and pepper. Dredge both sides of chicken in flour, and shake briefly so only a thin coating remains.
3. In a large sauté pan over medium-high heat, heat oil until it Shimmers. Lay chicken in hot oil (they should sizzle). Brown one side, turn with tongs, then brown other side.
4. Carefully add wine to pan—stand back, it may spatter!—and cover immediately. Reduce heat to medium and cook 3 to 5 minutes, or until juices run clear when a breast is poked at its thickest spot with the point of a knife. Remove chicken and drain on paper towels to blot excess oil. Discard pan juices.
5. Serve immediately, with the sauce on the side.

   Note:
   + If you want to serve chicken up to 30 minutes later, drain on paper towels as above, then place in a baking pan. Warm in preheated 400° oven 4 to 5 minutes before serving.

Browned-garlic butter sauce

Makes about 1½ cups sauce

2 teaspoons cornstarch
1 cup dry white wine
2 tablespoons canola or olive oil
¼ cup minced fresh garlic
8 ounces (2 sticks) unsalted butter, cut into chunks
1 teaspoon kosher salt
¼ teaspoon sugar
1 teaspoon seasoned rice wine vinegar

1. Measure all ingredients and place them next to the stove. Whisk cornstarch and wine together in a small bowl. In a medium saucepan, heat oil over medium-high heat until it shimmers. Add garlic and stir constantly with a metal or wooden spatula, scraping the pan as you go, until garlic is medium brown. Do not overcook.
2. Add the wine mixture immediately to the pan and whisk rapidly. Boil and whisk 30 seconds, or until sauce begins to thicken, then reduce heat to very low. Whisk in butter a chunk or two at a time.
3. Remove from heat and add salt, sugar, and vinegar. Mix well. Keep the sauce warm until serving.

   Notes:
   + Try this sauce with sautéed tofu or duck breasts.
   + Make a lemon-garlic variation for fish by omitting the rice wine vinegar and adding ¼ cup lemon juice at the end.
   + If you're a garlic lover, add 2 additional teaspoons minced fresh garlic along with other ingredients at the last step.

Buttermilk mashed potatoes

Mashed potatoes always elicit smiles. "Mashers" can be flavored in many ways: with chopped green onions, your favorite cheese, caramelized onions, braised garlic, or truffle oil. The buttermilk and sour cream lighten this version considerably; for a richer variation, substitute whipping cream for the buttermilk and butter for the sour cream.

Serves 6 to 8

1 tablespoon plus 1 teaspoon kosher salt, divided
8 large russet potatoes (about 3 pounds), peeled and cut into ½-inch chunks
1½ cups buttermilk
½ cup sour cream
¼ teaspoon white pepper

1. Bring about 3 quarts water and 1 tablespoon kosher salt to a boil in a large pot. Add potatoes and bring to a boil. Reduce heat to medium and simmer 8 to 12 minutes, until potatoes start to fall apart.
2. Drain potatoes well in a colander, then place in a large mixing bowl. Add buttermilk, sour cream, 1 teaspoon kosher salt, and pepper, and mash well with a potato masher.

   Notes:
   + Potatoes can also be whipped in a stand mixer. This results in the smoothest potatoes. They should be very hot, and whipped just until smooth. If overwhipped, they become "gluey," due to their high starch content.
   + This recipe is based on russet 80-count potatoes (80 indicates the number per box), a standard baking size. Many other types of potatoes can be used, such as Yukon Golds, red or "new" potatoes, and even purple potatoes.

Green beans with easy miso sauce

This recipe is one I use a lot, because the sauce goes well with a variety of dishes and it's so easy! The high-heat cooking gives extra color and flavor to the beans.

Serves 6 to 8

Miso sauce (recipe follows)
2 teaspoons kosher salt
1 pound fresh green beans (preferably Blue Lake) or yellow wax beans
2 tablespoons canola oil

1. Make **Miso sauce.**
2. Boil 1 gallon of water with the salt. Add beans and blanch 6 to 7 minutes, just until tender. Remove beans from water and drain well in a colander.
3. Heat oil in a large sauté pan until almost smoking. Add beans and cook until slightly brown, about 10 seconds. Turn a few times, then add miso sauce all at once. Stir well and remove from heat.

   Notes:
   + It's easy to prepare this side dish ahead of time: After blanching the beans, plunge them into ice water. When beans are cold, drain them well. To finish, proceed to last step.
   + This dish gets even better with the addition of other flavors. Try browned garlic (for method, see **Braised chard with browned garlic**), fresh ginger, red chile flakes, toasted sliced almonds, a dash of seasoned rice wine vinegar, or a combination of these ingredients.

Miso sauce

½ cup red miso
½ cup water or dry white wine

1. Place miso and water in a blender. Blend until smooth, about 6 seconds. If sauce seems too thick, add a little water.

Green salad
with candied pecans and pear-sherry dressing

The light dressing for this salad is a great way to use an overripe pear. After making the dressing, it's easy to adjust the flavor with more vinegar, or add a little more oil for a thicker consistency.

Serves 6 to 8

¾ pound mesclun mix or mixed baby greens
Pear and sherry dressing (recipe follows)
2 ripe d'Anjou, Bosc, or Asian pears, peeled and cut into ½-inch cubes
¾ cup **Candied pecans** (recipe follows)

1. Toss salad greens with just enough dressing to coat lightly.
2. Arrange greens on plates with pears and pecans.

Pear and sherry dressing

Makes 1½ cups

1 very ripe medium-size d'Anjou or Bosc pear
¼ cup good sherry vinegar
¼ cup water
1 tablespoon lemon juice
½ teaspoon kosher salt
¼ teaspoon black pepper
½ cup good olive oil

1. Peel and core pear. Place pear, vinegar, water, lemon juice, salt, and pepper in a blender. Blend 10 seconds, or until smooth.
2. With the motor running, add oil in a thin stream until it is fully incorporated. (See Emulsify in Resources: Glossary.)

Candied pecans

This recipe makes more than you'll need for the salad, but these shiny, crunchy nuts are quite habit-forming. Place any extras in a jar with a tight-fitting lid and use on cheese trays, or chop and serve with vanilla ice cream.

Makes 2 cups

½ cup powdered sugar
½ teaspoon kosher salt
¼ cup molasses
1 tablespoon water
½ teaspoon vanilla extract
2 cups pecan halves or pieces

1. Preheat oven to 350°.
2. Mix sugar, salt, molasses, water, and vanilla in a medium bowl. Add pecans and mix well to coat completely.
3. Lightly oil a baking pan and spread pecans on it. Bake 10 minutes, move pecans around on pan to cook evenly, and bake another 6 to 8 minutes. Molasses mix will be very thick and bubbly. Scrape nuts and all the caramel onto another lightly oiled pan to cool.

Poppy seed angel food cake
with orange-lime curd

Light as a cloud and fat-free—angel food, indeed. You'll need a 10-inch tube pan with a removable bottom for this recipe.

Makes 12 servings

2 cups egg whites, at room temperature (from about 14 eggs)
2 teaspoons lemon juice
1 tablespoon vanilla extract
½ teaspoon almond extract (optional)
2 cups sugar
½ teaspoon kosher salt
1¾ cups all-purpose or cake flour
4 tablespoons poppy seeds
Grated zest of 1 lemon (optional)
Orange-lime curd (recipe follows)

1. Preheat oven to 375°. Prepare the cake pan: Put a few drops of vegetable oil on your fingers and lightly spread it on the inside bottom ring of the pan. Do not oil the sides of the pan. (If the pan is too well lubricated, the cake will pull away as it cools and lose its shape.)
2. With an electric mixer, whip egg whites, lemon juice, and vanilla (and almond extract, if using) on high speed to soft-peak stage. Gradually add sugar and salt, and whip to stiff-peak stage.
3. Sift flour. Add poppy seeds and zest, if using. Fold half of flour mixture into the meringue, then fold in other half. Pour batter into pan and, with a knife or rubber spatula, spread batter so it is level.
4. Bake 25 to 30 minutes. While cake is baking, make **Orange-lime curd.**
5. Cake is done when the top is golden brown. The center will spring back when touched lightly, and a skewer inserted in the middle will come out dry. The cake may be puffy and cracked on top, or even slightly fallen (it will fall a bit anyway as it cools). Remove from oven and cool, upside down on a rack, for at least 15 minutes. Use a paring knife to cut the cake away from the pan.
6. Invert cake onto a serving plate. Cut cake with a serrated knife and serve with some of the **Orange-lime curd.**

Note:
+ Do not move a cake directly from the oven to a very cold place, or it will fall.

Orange-lime curd

Makes 1½ cups

½ cup lime juice
½ cup orange juice
1 egg
6 egg yolks
½ cup sugar
Pinch of kosher salt

1. Pour about ¾ inch water in the bottom of a double boiler, making certain top pan will not touch water. Bring the water to a boil, then reduce heat to simmer.
2. Combine lime juice, orange juice, egg, egg yolks, sugar, and salt in top of double boiler and whisk until smooth; set over the boiling water.
3. Cook over low heat 10 to 15 minutes, whisking curd occasionally as it thickens. Using a rubber spatula, push curd through a mesh strainer. Lightly press plastic wrap onto the surface of the curd to prevent a skin from forming on top. Refrigerate 30 minutes, or until cool.

Notes:
+ Turn this curd into a sauce by whisking in a little water.
+ To make Meyer lemon curd, omit both lime and orange juices, and use 1 cup Meyer lemon juice instead.
+ To make a lime- or lemon-only curd, omit orange juice, use 1 cup of lime or lemon juice, and increase sugar to 1 cup.
+ Curd can be thickened and used as a cake filling: whisk 2 teaspoons cornstarch into the lemon juice–egg mixture before heating it. Try this curd instead of the coconut custard in the **Sponge cake with coconut custard**.
+ You can lighten the texture of this curd by folding in **Sweetened whipped cream**. Mix 2 parts curd with 1 part whipped cream.

Easter Brunch

Easter, originally the pagan holiday of Eastre, commemorates the arrival of spring and new life. Today's Christian holiday is often celebrated with a brunch, perhaps because many people enjoy a late breakfast after church.

SUNDAY IN MARCH OR APRIL (DATE VARIES)

Asparagus-spinach soup

Smoked salmon and cream
cheese blintzes

Egg strata with sourdough bread,
spinach, Gruyère, and caramelized
onions

Spring garden salad
with fresh herbs

Fallen lemon soufflé cakes
with custard sauce

Asparagus-spinach soup

Potatoes provide a silky medium for the "green" flavors of asparagus and spinach in this spring soup.

Serves 8/Makes 8 cups

2 pounds asparagus
½ large onion, chopped (about 1 cup)
1 cup dry white wine
6 cups vegetable stock*
2 medium red potatoes, peeled and roughly chopped (about 1½ cups)
¼ pound fresh spinach
1 tablespoon kosher salt
½ teaspoon sugar
1 teaspoon white wine vinegar

1. Bend asparagus stalks until they break easily. Discard the bottom (tougher) parts and roughly chop the remainder.
2. Place onion and wine in a medium saucepan and bring to a boil. Boil for 1 minute to burn off alcohol. Add stock and asparagus and bring to a boil; reduce heat and simmer, covered, 10 minutes.
3. Add potatoes, bring back to a boil and simmer, covered, 10 minutes, or until very soft. Stir in spinach and let sit for 1 minute. Add salt, sugar, and vinegar.
4. In blender, purée in batches, filling container no more than half full each time and covering blender with a cloth to prevent hot mixture from spraying. Pour through a coarse strainer. Adjust seasonings as desired.

As a quick substitute for vegetable stock, try vegetarian chicken broth mix, available in the bulk foods section of natural foods stores. Whisk in 1 tablespoon for each cup of hot water.

Notes:
+ Fresh spinach must be washed thoroughly. Frozen, thawed spinach can be substituted for fresh spinach.
+ This soup can be served with croutons or a dollop of flavored cream (such as lemon juice added to sour cream). Chives, basil, or oregano can also be used to flavor the cream.
+ Try drizzling white truffle oil on the soup just before serving. If possible, select an oil with truffle "essence" instead of "aroma" or "flavoring."

Smoked salmon
and cream cheese blintzes

For this dish I like to use a French-style crêpe, which is slightly thinner than the traditional pancake used to make blintzes. Crisp from frying and filled with lemony cream cheese and smoked salmon, these blintzes disappeared quickly a few years ago when I served them to chefs and food writers at the Culinary Institute of America in Napa Valley.

Serves 8 to 10/Makes 25 to 30 filled blintzes

3 eggs
1½ cups milk
½ cup whipping cream
2 tablespoons canola oil
¼ cup water
Pinch of salt
1½ cups all-purpose flour
1 pound cream cheese, softened
3 tablespoons lemon juice
8 ounces sliced smoked salmon or salmon pieces
Canola oil, vegetable cooking spray, or DRAWN BUTTER (see Glossary)

1. Place eggs, milk, cream, oil, water, and salt in a blender. Blend about 4 seconds, or until smooth. Sift flour into a bowl and make a well in the center. Pour blended mixture into the well, then whisk until smooth. Let rest in the refrigerator for 30 minutes.
2. Make filling by mixing cream cheese with lemon juice until smooth.
3. Heat a nonstick crêpe pan or small frying pan over medium-high heat until very hot. Spray or lightly oil the pan. Make a test crêpe by pouring ¼ cup batter into pan and rolling the batter around the pan until it covers the bottom and the crêpe is as thin as possible. (If batter seems too thick, add a little water to batter in bowl.) Cook crêpe on one side until light brown, flip once, and after a few seconds turn out onto a plate.
4. Repeat process until all batter is used. Place a parchment paper square between every 4 crêpes to keep them from sticking together.
5. Lay 4 crêpes on a clean, dry work surface. Place 1 heaping tablespoon filling and a small slice of smoked salmon near the bottom edge of each crêpe. Fold the sides over the filling and salmon, and roll up the crêpe, starting at the bottom. Seal with a small dab of cream cheese filling. Press lightly to flatten a bit. Crêpes should look like tiny flattened burritos. Repeat the process until all ingredients are used.
6. Pour ⅛ inch oil into a large frying pan over medium heat and heat until oil SHIMMERS. Place 4 filled crêpes at a time in pan, seam side down, and cook until browned on both sides, about 2 minutes per side, turning once. (At this point, your crêpes become blintzes.) Remove from pan and drain on paper towels.

continued⟶

Smoked salmon
and cream cheese blintzes

continued from previous page

Notes:

- Cream cheese can be softened quickly in a microwave after removing from aluminum wrapper. Try warming 10 seconds at a time on high power until very soft.
- Blintzes can be made ahead and reheated in a 350° oven 5 minutes, or until heated through.
- Crêpes can be stored in a plastic zip-top bag and frozen for up to a month.
- Try filling crêpes with raspberry jam, sweetened cream cheese and blueberries, or whipped cream and chocolate sauce or Nutella. Crêpes can also be stacked, with **Coconut custard** spread between each one; cut into wedges to serve.
- To make fresh-herb crêpes, add 1 tablespoon chopped dill and ½ cup each finely chopped parsley and green onions to the batter. The herbs make each crêpe more attractive and flavorful.

Egg strata with sourdough bread,
spinach, Gruyère cheese, and caramelized onions

This dish borrows something from quiches, frittatas, and even upside-down cakes. The savory French toast is simpler to make than a pastry crust, and it gives the finished dish an attractive layered presentation. Factor in melted cheese, soft onions, herbs, and spinach, and you've got one hard-to-resist brunch dish.

Serves 8

1 cup **Caramelized onions** (page 195)
8 eggs
1 teaspoon granulated garlic
2 teaspoons kosher salt
1 teaspoon black pepper
¼ teaspoon cayenne pepper
1 teaspoon dried oregano
1 teaspoon dried thyme
2 cups half-and-half
6 slices sourdough bread
6 ounces grated Gruyère cheese (about 1½ cups)
½ pound frozen spinach, thawed and squeezed dry

1. Prepare **Caramelized onions**; set aside. Preheat oven to 350°.
2. Cut a square of parchment paper to fit inside an 8-by-8-inch baking pan. Lightly oil the pan, lay the parchment paper in the bottom, and lightly oil the paper.
3. Crack eggs into a medium mixing bowl and add garlic, salt, pepper, cayenne, oregano, and thyme. Whisk together. Heat half-and-half until almost boiling and slowly pour into the egg mixture, whisking constantly.
4. Place bread slices in baking pan, covering the bottom completely. Pour about ½ of the egg mixture over the bread. Sprinkle grated cheese over the bread in an even layer, all the way to the edges of the pan. Repeat with the caramelized onions, then the spinach. Pour the rest of the egg mixture over the spinach, to cover all the strata. Tap bottom of pan on work surface to release any bubbles. Let sit a few minutes and tap again.
5. Bake 50 minutes to 1 hour, until a knife inserted near center comes out dry and the top is browned. Cool 30 minutes. Run a paring knife around the edge of the pan and turn strata out onto a cutting board. Peel off parchment paper. Cut strata from corner to corner to make 4 triangles, then cut each triangle in half again to make 8.

   Notes:
   + A variety of cheeses can be used: try jack, pepper jack, Fontina, Cheddar, or softened cream cheese. Cheese mixtures are good, too: try half Gruyère and half Asiago.
   + Look for leaf spinach frozen loose in bags. Inexpensive boxed spinach can be tough and full of stems.

Spring garden salad
with fresh herbs

This salad is inspired by the farmers market. I love strolling by the booths, looking at the brightly colored fruits and vegetables, and sampling peak-of-season peaches, dried fruits, honey, nuts, and fresh herbs. Being a regular at the market enables me to get to know the purveyors, who like to share a joke or a little gossip and tell me what produce is coming in next. This recipe is very flexible: feel free to add or omit herbs.

Serves 8

¾ pound fresh baby spinach
½ cup Italian parsley leaves
¼ cup cilantro leaves
¼ cup mint leaves
½ cup basil leaves, roughly chopped
¼ cup chopped chives, or chive blossoms
1 tablespoon fresh oregano leaves
½ cup chervil leaves (optional)
Lemon dressing (recipe follows)

1. Combine greens and herbs in a salad bowl.
2. Toss greens with just enough dressing to coat lightly.

Lemon dressing

Makes about ½ cup

Very light and tart, this dressing enhances the other salad ingredients without stealing the show. Use it for any salad that is going to be served with rich dishes.

2 tablespoons lemon juice
2 tablespoons balsamic vinegar
½ teaspoon kosher salt
¼ teaspoon black pepper
4 tablespoons good olive oil

1. Place lemon juice, vinegar, salt, pepper, and oil in a jar with a tight-fitting lid.
2. Shake until well mixed.

Fallen lemon soufflé cakes
with custard sauce

Several years ago a popular food magazine published a soufflé recipe of mine. The photo shoot took two days and at least ten soufflés. This "fallen" version removes the pressure of perfect timing. A soufflé doesn't have to be right out of the oven to be great!

Serves 8

Lemon soufflé filling (recipe follows)
Custard sauce (recipe follows)
½ cup graham cracker crumbs
3 tablespoons unsalted butter, melted
2 tablespoons sugar

1. Make **Lemon soufflé filling** and **Custard sauce**.
2. Lightly oil the insides of 8 (6-ounce) ramekins or custard cups.
3. Make crust: Mix cracker crumbs, butter, and sugar thoroughly. Divide evenly among the ramekins and tamp bottom with a small can or a bottle with a flat surface.

   Notes:
   + If you're confident in your timing, you can make this recipe at the last minute and serve it immediately as a soufflé. Be aware: it will fall quickly.
   + The soufflé can be made without the graham cracker crust.
   + To make this recipe in a pie pan: double the amount of crust, tamp into bottom of a 9-inch pie pan, pour the filling into the pan, then bake as directed above. When cool, cut pie into 8 or 12 wedges and serve with custard sauce poured over each one.

Lemon soufflé filling

½ cup lemon juice
6 egg yolks
¾ cup sugar, divided
Pinch of salt
2 teaspoons cornstarch
5 egg whites, at room temperature

1. Preheat oven to 400°. Pour about ¾ inch water in the bottom of a double boiler, making certain top pan will not touch water. Combine lemon juice, egg yolks, ¼ cup of the sugar, salt, and cornstarch in top of double boiler and whisk until smooth.
2. Bring the water in the saucepan to a boil, then reduce heat to simmer. Place the bowl with the lemon mixture on top of the saucepan.
3. Cook over low heat for 8 minutes, whisking occasionally as mixture thickens. Remove from heat and set aside.

continued⟶

Fallen lemon soufflé cakes
with custard sauce

continued from previous page

4. Place egg whites in another metal mixing bowl and beat until frothy. Gradually beat in remaining ½ cup sugar on high speed with an electric mixer to soft-peak stage. FOLD half of the egg whites into the lemon mixture, FOLD in remaining half, and spoon into ramekins. Ramekins should be full.

5. Place ramekins in oven and bake 12 minutes or until soufflés are fully puffed and brown on top. Let cool until ready to serve (they will have fallen), then pour a few tablespoons of custard sauce on top of each one and serve.

Notes:
+ For a Meyer lemon version, substitute Meyer lemon juice for the lemon juice and reduce the sugar measurement in step 4 to ¼ cup.
+ An electric beater or stand mixer works best for whipping egg whites. They whip best when they are at room temperature or slightly warm.

Custard sauce

Traditionally, custard sauce, or crème anglaise, is cooked twice—which is tricky because the egg yolks can curdle. I learned the simple technique used here from a pastry chef in Lyon, France.

Makes 2 cups

5 egg yolks
1½ cups whipping cream
½ cup plus 2 tablespoons sugar
Pinch of kosher salt
1 teaspoon vanilla extract

1. Place egg yolks in a small bowl and set aside.
2. Place cream, sugar, and salt in a small, heavy saucepan and bring to a boil, stirring occasionally to dissolve sugar.
3. Remove from heat and immediately whisk about half of the hot cream mixture into the egg yolks. Add this mixture back into the hot cream in the saucepan. Whisk to combine, cover the pan, and let sit for 10 minutes.
4. Pour custard through mesh strainer, stir in vanilla, cover bowl with plastic wrap, and chill.

Notes:
+ Egg whites can be frozen in a plastic zip-top bag for later use.
+ Custard sauce can be made with half-and-half instead of cream, but it will not be quite as thick.
+ The degree of risk associated with harmful bacteria in raw eggs can vary. Use only raw eggs purchased from a reliable source. For more information, see the American Egg Board website, www.aeb.org.
+ Custard sauce is extremely versatile. Serve plain or flavor with coffee crystals, brandy, Frangelico, or Grand Marnier.

Cinco de Mayo Fiesta

MAY 5

On the fifth day of May, 1862, an outnumbered Mexican army defeated the French forces at Puebla. Although this battle did not gain independence for Mexico, many people in the United States observe Cinco de Mayo as if it were a Mexican Independence Day. Here are some ideas for your own celebration.

Chicken posole with traditional garnishes

Baked chiles rellenos with easy red sauce

Carrots with honey, butter, and cumin

Coleslaw with spicy cilantro dressing

Cornmeal cake with strawberries and their syrup

Chicken posole
with traditional garnishes

Traditionally, posole is made with pork. This version, made with chicken, is prized for its curative properties. My friends rely on me to deliver a batch on New Year's Day.

Serves 10 to 12/Makes 5 quarts

1 (3½- to 4-pound) chicken, cut into 8 pieces
2 cups **Chile purée** (recipe follows)
3½ quarts water
1½ cups diced yellow or red onion
¼ cup sliced garlic cloves (about 10)
2 tablespoons canola or salad oil
1 (14½-ounce) can diced tomatoes with their juice
1 (29-ounce) can golden hominy, rinsed and drained
1 teaspoon dried oregano
1 tablespoon plus 1 teaspoon kosher salt
1 teaspoon black pepper

Garnishes:
16 flour tortillas
1 cup diced red onion
1 cup roughly chopped cilantro (stems and leaves)
¼ cup seeded, minced jalapeño peppers
8 lime wedges (from 2 limes)

1. Remove and discard all chicken skin. Place chicken pieces in a medium stockpot with water and bring to a boil. Skim off any scum that collects on the surface. Reduce heat and simmer 15 to 20 minutes.
2. Make **Chile purée.**
3. Remove chicken stock from heat. Remove chicken pieces from broth, allow to cool, then pull all meat from bones and set it aside.
4. Place bones back in broth and bring to a boil; skim again, reduce heat, and simmer 20 minutes, covered. Strain broth and discard bones. Set broth aside.
5. In the same stockpot, heat oil over medium heat until it SHIMMERS. Add onion and garlic and stir for a few minutes, until onion is translucent. Add the chicken broth, chile purée, tomatoes, hominy, cooked chicken, oregano, salt, and pepper. Bring back to a boil, reduce heat, and simmer 5 minutes.
6. Meanwhile, warm tortillas in oven or microwave, or on griddle. Serve posole with tortillas and garnishes on the side.

Notes:
- **Three chile purée** can be substituted for the **Chile purée.**
- When cooking stock, position the pot on the stove so the burner is under one side of the pot; scum that rises will go to the other side of the pot, making it easier to skim. Always simmer stocks gently, as a full boil will make them cloudy.
- If you like spicy food, leave the seeds in the jalapeño peppers.
- Leftover posole is great warmed up the next day or two. It can be frozen for up to two months.
- For a light meal, serve posole with quesadillas and a tossed green salad.

Chile purée

Makes about 2 cups

¼ pound dried California, New Mexico, or Ancho chiles
2 cups water

1. Stem and seed chiles. Place them in a small pan with water and bring to a boil. Reduce heat and simmer, covered, 15 to 20 minutes.
2. Pour chile mixture into blender. Blend until smooth, about 10 seconds, covering blender with a cloth to prevent hot mixture from spraying. Push mixture through a mesh strainer. Rinse blender with an additional ½ cup water and pour through strainer. Discard pulp.

Baked chiles rellenos
with easy red sauce

My twist on this classic dish adds rice and quinoa to the cheese filling and eliminates the batter and deep frying.

Serves 8

3½ cups **Easy red sauce**, divided (recipe follows)
2 tablespoons canola oil
½ recipe (about 2½ cups) **Jasmine rice-quinoa pilaf** (page 49)
¾ pound jack cheese, cut into ½-inch cubes
10 poblano chiles

1. Make **Easy red sauce.**
2. Leaving stems of chiles attached and taking care not to open the chiles too much, roast, peel, and seed poblano chiles (for technique, see **Roasted peppers** in Essential Recipes). If you slice open the roasted chile lengthwise, you can usually remove the seeds without destroying the shape of the chile.
3. Combine pilaf and cheese cubes. Stuff 8 chiles with the mixture. (Two extra chiles are called for, in case some didn't survive the roasting and peeling procedure.)
4. Preheat oven to 375°. Lightly oil a 13-by-9-by-2-inch baking pan. Ladle 1½ cups of sauce into pan and place chiles in sauce. Ladle remaining 2 cups of sauce on top of chiles, or enough to cover them well. Cover pan with aluminum foil.
5. Bake chiles rellenos 25 to 30 minutes, until sauce bubbles and cheese is melted.

   Notes:
   + Poblano chiles are like jalapeños: the degree of spiciness varies. That is, they can be as mild as bell peppers or spicy as heck. If you prefer mild dishes, use a red bell pepper or a mild chile such as Anaheim.
   + You can use all quinoa or all rice if preferred; they cook in the same amount of time.
   + Chiles can be stuffed with any number of things: picadillo (a mixture of ground meat, raisins, and nuts); **Tamari-roasted pumpkinseeds** and pepper jack cheese; roasted vegetables, shellfish, scrambled eggs, or ground turkey.
   + Try pairing chiles with other sauces, such as **Mole poblano** or **Fresh tomato salsa**.

Easy red sauce

This is a good, quick sauce for rellenos and enchiladas. Red enchilada sauces do not usually have tomatoes in them, but I find that the tart sweetness of tomatoes complements the earthy flavor of the store-bought enchilada sauce.

Makes about 6 cups

2 tablespoons **Chipotle purée** (page 197), or 1 large canned chipotle chile
1 (28-ounce) can mild enchilada sauce
1 cup water
¾ cup chopped yellow onion
1 large red bell pepper, roughly chopped
7 cloves garlic
1 (8-ounce) can tomato sauce
2 teaspoons kosher salt
1 teaspoon sugar

1. Make **Chipotle purée**. Pour canned enchilada sauce into medium saucepan, rinse can with the water, and add water to saucepan. Add onion, bell pepper, garlic, chipotle purée, and tomato sauce. Bring mixture to a boil, lower heat, and simmer 15 to 20 minutes, stirring occasionally.
2. Purée mixture in batches in a blender on high speed until very smooth, covering blender with a cloth to prevent hot mixture from spraying.

Note:
+ Any canned enchilada sauce can be used. Las Palmas brand comes in mild, medium, and hot. If you choose the hot version, omit the chipotle purée.

Carrots with honey, butter, and cumin

With their rich, deep flavor and year-round availability, carrots deserve more starring roles. This recipe's sweet-sour balance, enhanced with cumin, plays nicely off the other dishes in this menu.

Serves 6 to 8

8 cups water
2½ teaspoons kosher salt, divided
2½ pounds carrots, peeled and cut into ½-inch slices
3 ounces (¾ stick) unsalted butter
¼ cup honey
1 teaspoon ground cumin
2 tablespoons lime juice

1. Bring water and 2 teaspoons of the salt to a boil in a large saucepan. Add carrots and cook 6 to 8 minutes, or until carrots are slightly softened.
2. Drain carrots well and put back into pan. Add butter, honey, cumin, lime juice, and remaining ½ teaspoon salt.
   Stir until butter is melted and carrots are well coated.

   Notes:
   + Some other ideas for flavoring carrots: ginger and honey, fennel seeds, red chile flakes, and lemon juice, or pomegranate molasses (available at Middle Eastern markets, or on the Internet; see Resources: Websites and Ordering Information).
   + If you like the flavors in this recipe, you can use them to make a COMPOUND BUTTER: Soften butter, then mix in the other ingredients (except the carrots). Roll in plastic wrap to form logs, label, and store in the refrigerator for up to 1 week or in the freezer for up to 2 months.

Coleslaw with spicy cilantro dressing

Here's a zesty twist on coleslaw: crunchy cabbage tossed with a hot-sweet cilantro dressing. Although it's practically unknown in Mexican cookery, I've found that rice wine vinegar is a "crossover" flavor that works well in both Asian and Latin dishes.

Serves 8

Spicy cilantro dressing (recipe follows)
8 cups thinly sliced napa or green cabbage (about a 2-pound cabbage)
1½ cups grated carrot
1 cup chopped green onion

1. Make **Spicy cilantro dressing.**
2. Combine vegetables with dressing. Serve within ½ hour.

Spicy cilantro dressing

Makes 1¾ cups

1½ cups chopped cilantro
½ cup chopped green onion
½ cup seasoned rice wine vinegar
1 tablespoon sugar
2 teaspoons kosher salt
1 jalapeño pepper, roughly chopped (with seeds)
¼ cup plus 1 tablespoon lime juice
2 teaspoons minced fresh garlic
½ cup canola oil

1. Place all ingredients except canola oil in a blender and blend on high speed for 5 seconds. With the motor running, add oil in a thin stream until it is fully incorporated. (See EMULSIFY in Resources: Glossary.)

Cornmeal cake
with strawberries and their syrup

Our guests (and staff) find this moist, grainy cake irresistible. In spring and summer I buy perfect strawberries from a stand near the Ranch and toss them with a little sugar, which creates a lovely syrup. I often serve the cornmeal cake with only a dusting of powdered sugar on top. Sometimes, though, I just can't resist adding the fluffy, lemon-scented frosting.

Makes 1 (9-inch round) 2-layer cake

6 eggs
½ pound (2 sticks) unsalted butter, melted
1¼ cups sugar
1¼ cups all-purpose flour
1 tablespoon baking powder
¼ teaspoon table salt
¾ cup cornmeal
5 egg yolks
2 teaspoons vanilla extract
¼ cup hot tap water
Lemon cream cheese frosting (recipe follows)
Strawberries and their syrup (recipe follows)

1. Preheat oven to 350°. Oil and flour two 9-inch round cake pans.
2. Place eggs, uncracked and in their shells, in a bowl. Cover with hot tap water and let sit for about 10 minutes; drain.
3. Combine butter and sugar in a bowl and mix well with a rubber spatula.
4. Sift flour, baking powder, and salt together. Stir cornmeal into flour mixture.
5. Crack the 6 eggs into a large mixing bowl; add yolks, vanilla, and the ¼ cup hot water. Beat the mixture at high speed of an electric mixer for 2 minutes. It should be very foamy but not thick.
6. Add butter mixture and flour mixture to egg mixture and fold together with a rubber spatula. Divide batter between prepared pans. The batter will fill each pan only halfway.
7. Bake cakes 30 minutes, or until the center springs back when touched lightly and a skewer inserted in the middle comes out dry. Cool cakes completely in pan.
8. Make **Lemon cream cheese frosting** and **Strawberries and their syrup.**
9. Use a paring knife to cut the cake away from the pan. Turn cake out onto a serving plate. Spread about half of frosting on top of one cake round. Place other cake round on top of frosting. Use remaining frosting to cover top and sides.
10. Cut cake into wedges and serve with a spoonful of berries and syrup on each plate.

Lemon cream cheese frosting

Makes 3 cups

8 ounces cream cheese
½ pound (2 sticks) unsalted butter
1 cup powdered sugar, sifted
2 teaspoons lemon zest (from 1 lemon)
1 tablespoon lemon juice (from ½ lemon)
1 teaspoon vanilla extract

1. Place cream cheese and butter in a glass mixing bowl and microwave in 20-second increments until they are very soft but not melted.
2. Add remaining ingredients and whisk rapidly for 20 to 30 seconds, or until very fluffy.

Strawberries and their syrup

Makes 2 cups

2 (1-pint) baskets strawberries
3 tablespoons sugar

1. Wash and stem the berries, then cut in half lengthwise. Toss berries with sugar at least 30 minutes, or up to 2 hours, before serving.

Memorial Day Picnic

On this holiday, Americans take time to honor those who gave their all for our country. Here are some portable dishes for your picnic basket. Remember to pack extra bowls for tossing the Caesar salad at the last minute and giving the chicken a final coating with barbecue sauce.

Chipotle barbecued chicken

Yukon Gold potato salad with Dijon dressing, celery, and capers

Classic Caesar salad

Zucchini gratin Provençal

Granola cookies

Chipotle barbecued chicken

Barbecue can refer either to a cooking method or to a sauce. Here, it refers to the sauce, which, combined with the spice rub and overnight marinating technique, produces a real finger-lickin' chicken.

Serves 8

2 tablespoons **New Mexico spice mix** (recipe follows)
1 tablespoon kosher salt, divided
2 (2½- to 3-pound) chickens, each cut into 8 pieces
2½ cups **Chipotle barbecue sauce** (recipe follows), divided

1. Combine spice mix and 2 teaspoons of the salt. Sprinkle chicken pieces with mixture, coating well.
   Cover and let sit 15 minutes. Add 2 cups of the barbecue sauce and turn chicken pieces to coat, then cover and refrigerate overnight.
2. Preheat oven to 400°.
3. Season chicken pieces with the remaining teaspoon of salt, place on an oiled baking pan, and roast in oven 15 minutes, or until chicken is cooked to the bone (juices will run clear when poked in thickest point with a knife tip). Remove chicken pieces from pan and discard juices.
4. Coat chicken pieces with the remaining ½ cup barbecue sauce just before serving.

   Notes:
   + If you don't have all the ingredients for the spice mix, the chicken is still delicious without it.
   + When you marinate the chicken overnight, the flavor goes all the way to the bone.
     If you are in a hurry, marinate the chicken in the morning and cook it that night.
   + Die-hard grilling fans can combine the marinating technique here with the cooking method for **Grill-smoked salmon**. Remember to oil the grill lightly and to let the coals burn down to white with no flames, or the chicken will burn. I like to cover the grill after turning the chicken so it is more like an oven, with heat all around the chicken.

New Mexico spice mix
Keep this blend on hand for steak, tofu brochettes, or grilled vegetables.

Makes ¾ cup plus 2 tablespoons

1½ tablespoons ground cumin
2 tablespoons ground coriander
1 tablespoon granulated garlic
1 tablespoon onion powder
2 tablespoons paprika
1 teaspoon cayenne pepper
1½ tablespoons dried oregano
2 tablespoons kosher salt
1 tablespoon black pepper
2 tablespoons chili powder

1. Mix all ingredients well. Store leftover spice mix in a jar with a lid.

Chipotle barbecue sauce

Sweet, sour, hot, smoky, and a snap to make. Who needs to buy barbecue sauce from a store?

Makes 6 cups

¼ cup **Chipotle purée** (recipe follows)
½ cup cider vinegar
1 quart ketchup
¼ cup soy sauce
¼ cup molasses
¼ cup lightly packed light brown sugar
2 teaspoons granulated garlic
2 teaspoons granulated onion
2 teaspoons black pepper
1 teaspoon white pepper
½ cup orange juice

1. Make **Chipotle purée**.
2. Whisk all ingredients together well.

    Notes:
    + This sauce keeps for at least two weeks in the refrigerator. It will thicken as it sits; to thin, whisk in a little water.
    + This sauce can be habit-forming. Try serving it with pork or brushing it on salmon steaks before grilling.

Chipotle purée

Makes about 1¼ cups

1 (7-ounce) can chipotle chiles in adobo sauce
Water

1. Place contents of can in a blender. Add water to the can until it is about ⅔ full. Swirl water around can to rinse well, then pour into blender.
2. Blend on high speed 10 seconds, or until completely smooth.

    Note:
    + Use leftover purée on quesadillas, in almost any kind of salsa, and for rubs and marinades. Refrigerate, or freeze extra purée in an ice cube tray; transfer frozen cubes to a zip-top plastic bag.

Yukon Gold potato salad
with Dijon dressing, celery, and capers

As a cooking student, I was researching potato salad recipes one day in the San Francisco Public Library. Seeking something lighter than the traditional mayonnaise-and-hard-boiled-egg type, I discovered a recipe with cucumbers. These days, I add even more crunch with celery and capers.

Serves 8

1 tablespoon kosher salt
2½ pounds Yukon Gold potatoes
Dijon dressing (recipe follows)
2 stalks celery, diced
2 tablespoons capers
½ cup chopped Italian parsley
½ English cucumber, cut in ½-inch cubes

1. In a large pot, bring salt and 1 gallon water to a boil.
2. Wash potatoes (do not peel) and cut into ¾-inch cubes. Add to boiling water and cook until just soft, about 8 minutes. Drain well and spread out on a baking pan to cool.
3. Make **Dijon dressing**.
4. Place potatoes, celery, capers, parsley, and cucumber in a large mixing bowl. Add the dressing and toss to coat.

Dijon dressing

Makes 2 cups

½ cup smooth Dijon-style mustard
¼ cup cider, white-wine, or tarragon vinegar
2 teaspoons kosher salt
1 teaspoon black pepper
⅓ cup water
½ teaspoon ground celery seeds
1½ cups good olive oil

1. Place all ingredients except oil in a blender or food processor. Blend a few seconds, until well mixed.
2. With the motor running, add oil in a thin stream until it is fully incorporated. (See Emulsify in Resources: Glossary.)

   Note:
   + The dressing may taste salty, but potatoes absorb salt quickly. If the potato salad sits more than a few hours before serving, taste and add more salt as desired.

Classic Caesar salad

After sampling many a Caesar salad in restaurants far and wide, and making the dressing many times myself, I arrived at this version and stopped tweaking it.

Serves 8/dressing makes 1¾ cups

2 tablespoons minced fresh garlic
1 cup freshly grated Parmesan cheese, divided
1 tablespoon Worchestershire sauce
¼ cup red wine vinegar
2 tablespoons lemon juice
1 egg yolk
2 teaspoons anchovy paste or minced canned anchovies
1 teaspoon kosher salt
1 teaspoon black pepper
1 cup good olive oil
3 hearts of romaine lettuce (prewashed)
Easy garlic croutons (recipe follows)

1. Place garlic, ½ cup of the parmesan cheese, the Worchestershire sauce, vinegar, lemon juice, egg yolk, anchovy paste, salt, and pepper in a blender or food processor. Blend until smooth, about 10 seconds. With the motor running, add oil in a thin stream until it is fully incorporated. (See Emulsify in Resources: Glossary.)
2. Cut each romaine head in half lengthwise, keeping core attached. Slice into ¾-inch chunks. Discard core.
3. For picnic, transfer romaine to plastic zip-top bag and toss with dressing, remaining ½ cup of cheese, and croutons at picnic site; to serve immediately, toss lettuce, remaining ½ cup cheese, and croutons with enough dressing to coat well. A Caesar is one of the few salads that's best a little overdressed.

Notes:
+ If you can find anchovies packed in salt, use them instead of anchovy paste. Anchovies packed in salt should be rinsed before using.
+ Asiago cheese can be substituted for Parmesan cheese.
+ Leftover dressing can be refrigerated for up to four days. Try using it instead of mayonnaise on a sandwich.
+ The degree of risk associated with harmful bacteria in raw eggs can vary. Use only raw eggs purchased from a reliable source. For more information, see the American Egg Board website, www.aeb.org.
+ This recipe makes about twice as much dressing as you'll need to dress the greens, for two reasons: blenders need a certain amount of liquid to function correctly, and the amount of liquid flavorings this dressing contains requires a full cup of oil to thicken properly.
+ Hearts of romaine are usually prewashed. If in doubt, cut lettuce, wash, and spin dry.
+ Anchovy or garlic lovers may desire an extra teaspoon of one or both of these ingredients.

continued⟶

Classic Caesar salad

continued from previous page

Easy garlic croutons

Makes 3 cups

½ pound bread, cut into ½-inch cubes
2 tablespoons good olive oil
¼ teaspoon kosher salt
⅛ teaspoon black pepper
1 teaspoon granulated garlic

1. Preheat oven to 325°.
2. Place bread cubes in a large mixing bowl. Drizzle cubes with oil, tossing cubes so the oil is evenly distributed. Add seasonings in the same manner. Spread cubes in a single layer on a baking pan. Bake 8 minutes, then stir croutons to ensure even browning. Bake 8 to 10 minutes more, or until croutons are light brown, very dry, and crisp.

   Notes:
   + I like a good sourdough bread for croutons, crust and all, but almost any type of bread can be used.
   + Granulated garlic is slightly yellower and coarser than powdered, with the real flavor of garlic.

Zucchini gratin Provençal

This casserole blends the garlic, olive oil, and tomatoes of France's sunny southern region. Enjoy it year-round: in cold weather, serve piping hot; in warm weather, serve at room temperature.

Serves 8

5 medium green zucchini, sliced in thin rounds
1 small yellow onion, thinly sliced
2 tablespoons minced fresh garlic
¼ cup plus 2 tablespoons good olive oil
2 teaspoons kosher salt
½ teaspoon black pepper
½ cup freshly grated Asiago or Parmesan cheese
5 fresh plum or Roma tomatoes, sliced in thin rounds

1. Lightly oil an 8-by-8-by 2-inch baking pan. Preheat oven to 375°.
2. Toss all ingredients together in a large mixing bowl. Pack mixture into the baking pan— it will be very full. Cover pan with foil and bake 1½ hours, until vegetables are very soft.
3. Cool gratin 10 minutes and then press another pan or plate down on top of the foil. Hold pans together and carefully tilt over the sink, draining excess juice until very little liquid comes out, about 5 seconds. This process also presses the gratin flat, which creates a nicer presentation.
4. Remove foil, cut gratin into 8 portions, and serve.

    Notes:
    + In summer, add ¼ cup chopped fresh basil to other ingredients in mixing bowl.
    + This is a great side dish for many meals: try it with chicken, beef, or pork dishes. For a vegetarian meal, serve with rice and a green salad.
    + Any type of tomato can be used in this recipe.
    + Many gratins are topped with bread crumbs. This one can be prepared the same way: just sprinkle about ½ cup of dry white bread crumbs on top before baking. Remove foil during the last 5 minutes of baking to brown. The crumbs help absorb excess juice.

Granola cookies

Like a bowl of granola, these cookies are full of oats, dried fruit, and coconut. Like all good cookies, they're great any time of day.

50 small cookies

½ pound unsalted butter, softened
1 cup lightly packed light brown sugar
½ cup sugar
2 eggs
3 cups rolled oats
1½ cups all-purpose flour
½ teaspoon ground nutmeg
¼ teaspoon table salt
½ teaspoon baking soda
2 teaspoons ground ginger
¾ cup chopped walnuts
½ cup raisins
1 cup dried cranberries
1 cup sweetened flaked coconut

1. Preheat oven to 350°.
2. Combine butter and sugars in a mixing bowl and beat with an electric mixer until creamy. Add eggs and beat well.
3. "PULSE" the oatmeal briefly in a food processor until roughly chopped (or chop on a cutting board with a knife). Do not process too long. Sift together the flour, nutmeg, salt, baking soda, and ginger. Add to the egg mixture with the oatmeal, walnuts, raisins, cranberries, and coconut. Mix together with a rubber spatula or wooden spoon just until combined.
4. Scoop heaping tablespoons of dough onto an oiled or parchment paper–lined baking pan. Wet fingers and press each cookie until slightly flattened.
5. Bake 10 minutes, or until cookies are lightly browned all over. Do not overbake.

Note:
+ This is a wonderful "base" recipe. Have fun and experiment with substitutions for the last four ingredients. For example, try chocolate chips instead of walnuts. Any type of dried fruit can be used in place of the raisins and cranberries.

Summer Menus

Mediterranean
Summer Solstice Party

Eclectic Independence Day
Dinner

Bastille Day Celebration

Birthday Party at the Beach

Mediterranean Summer Solstice Party

JUNE 21

Solstice: literally, sun standing still. The sun is at its highest point in the sky, summer gardens are ripening, and school is out for the summer. The Westerbekes often celebrate by throwing a party. They invite lots of friends, build a bonfire down near the garden, have a relaxed dinner, play music, and sometimes dance until the wee hours.

White fish with
saffron-tomato sauce

Jasmine rice–quinoa pilaf

Chayote putanesca

Roasted ratatouille

Green salad with roasted beets,
Mezzo Secco cheese, and
red pepper–sherry dressing

Raspberry pizza

White fish with saffron-tomato sauce

This sauce is great with almost any type of white fish. Try tilapia, snapper, sea bass, or cod.

Serves 8

Saffron-tomato sauce (recipe follows)
8 (6-ounce) halibut steaks
2 tablespoons chopped Italian parsley, for garnish

1. Make **Saffron-tomato sauce.**
2. Preheat oven to 375°. Lightly oil a 13-by-9-by-2-inch baking pan.
3. Lay fish in the baking pan. They can touch but should not overlap. Ladle sauce over fish, making sure to cover each piece with some sauce. Bake, uncovered, 15 minutes, or until fish flakes easily with a fork. Place fish on a platter and top with some of the warm sauce from the pan. Sprinkle with parsley and serve.

   Notes:
   + Capers are a nice addition to this sauce. If desired, add 1 tablespoon capers when you add the salt, pepper, and other seasonings.
   + Use an electric spice or coffee mill to grind the fennel seeds.
   + I usually serve 5 to 6 ounces of fish per person. Tilapia filets are about 8 ounces each, so I cut them in half. Light eaters can have one piece; bigger appetites, two. When purchasing fish, consider your guests' appetites and what else is being served. If in doubt, buy extra so no one leaves hungry.

Saffron-tomato sauce

2 tablespoons canola oil
½ cup thinly sliced yellow onion
2 tablespoons minced fresh garlic
¼ teaspoon saffron threads, crushed
½ cup dry white wine
1 cup canned or bottled clam juice
¾ cup canned diced tomatoes in their juice
½ teaspoon kosher salt
½ teaspoon black pepper
¼ teaspoon red chile flakes
½ teaspoon fennel seeds, roughly ground

1. Heat oil in a medium saucepan over medium heat until it SHIMMERS. Add onion and cook, stirring frequently, until translucent. Add garlic and saffron, and sauté a minute or so. Add wine and boil about 4 minutes to burn off alcohol and reduce a bit. Add clam juice and tomatoes, and simmer 5 minutes, uncovered. Add salt, pepper, chile flakes, and fennel seeds, and simmer 2 more minutes. Remove from heat and let sit for 15 minutes.

Jasmine rice–quinoa pilaf

Many cultures have a version of pilaf made with grains (usually rice) and other ingredients. This version uses flavorful jasmine rice and quinoa, a high-protein grain originally grown in the Andes. Here, the two are teamed up with aromatic vegetables for a nutritious side dish.

Serves 6 to 8/Makes about 5 cups

3 tablespoons canola oil
¾ cup jasmine rice
¾ cup quinoa
½ cup finely chopped carrot
½ cup finely chopped yellow onion
1 tablespoon minced fresh garlic
2½ cups vegetable stock*
1 teaspoon kosher salt

1. Heat oil in a medium saucepan over medium-high heat until it SHIMMERS. Add rice and cook, stirring frequently, until grains start to brown, about 5 minutes.
2. Add quinoa, carrot, onion, and garlic, stir for another minute, then add stock and salt. Stir together. Bring to a boil, reduce heat to low, cover, and cook 15 minutes.
3. Remove from heat and let sit 5 minutes, covered. Fluff with a fork before serving.

* As a quick substitute for vegetable stock, try vegetarian chicken broth mix, available in the bulk foods section of natural foods stores. Whisk in 1 tablespoon for each cup of hot water.

Notes:
  + Many things can be incorporated into a pilaf. Try raisins or other dried fruit, toasted nuts or seeds, chopped green onions, or chopped parsley; add at step 3 and let steam 5 minutes, as described above. Cut-up chicken, lamb, or pork can be SEARED, then simmered with the grains in step 1, for a one-pot meal; or add cooked meat or poultry leftovers at step 3.
  + Browning the grains in oil before boiling gives this side dish a wonderful, nutty flavor and keeps the grains fluffy and separate. For a milder flavor, do not brown the grains, stir all ingredients together, and cook as directed above.

Chayote putanesca

Putanesca is typically a preparation for pasta, with a suggestive name that refers to harried "working girls." I've replaced the pasta with chayote, a wonderful, juicy vegetable in the gourd family. In Louisiana, where it is called mirliton, it is often stuffed and baked.

Serves 8

4 chayotes
2 tablespoons olive oil
⅓ cup diced yellow onion
1 tablespoon minced fresh garlic
½ cup dry white wine
1 tablespoon plus 2 teaspoons capers
1 tablespoon caper juice
¼ teaspoon red chile flakes
½ cup canned diced tomatoes in their juice
1 teaspoon kosher salt
¼ teaspoon black pepper

1. Peel and cut chayotes in ½- to ¾-inch cubes. Do not remove the pit, as it is edible and has a pleasantly nutty flavor. Cook cubes in a generous amount of boiling salted water until al dente (4 to 6 minutes). Drain, spread on a baking pan, and cool.
2. In a medium sauté pan over medium-high heat, heat olive oil until it SHIMMERS. Add onion and garlic, and sauté until translucent. Add wine and cook until liquid is reduced by half. Add capers, caper juice, chile flakes, tomatoes, salt, and pepper. Simmer 5 minutes.
3. Add chayote and heat through. Remove pan from heat, cover, and let sit 10 minutes or until ready to serve.

   Notes:
   + Wash your hands well after peeling and cutting chayote, as it will coat your skin with a gluey substance. If working with large amounts, wear gloves.
   + Chayote absorbs flavors beautifully, so this dish just gets better as it sits. Make it early on and let the flavors marinate. Serve warm, or at room temperature in hot weather.
   + When BLANCHING vegetables it's common to SHOCK them in ice water to stop the cooking; but chayote is much more forgiving of a little overcooking than, say, broccoli. Also, letting the chayote (or any vegetable) cool without shocking it retains more flavor.

Roasted ratatouille

I've modified the Provençal classic by roasting most of the ingredients instead of stewing them. Serve ratatouille warm or at room temperature. Since basil is grown in hothouses in the winter, this easy dish can be served year-round.

Serves 8

1½ pounds eggplant
2 teaspoons kosher salt, divided
1½ teaspoons black pepper, divided
½ cup plus 2 tablespoons good olive oil, divided
5 medium green or yellow zucchini, cut into ½-inch rounds or wedges
5 fresh Roma tomatoes (about 1 pound), quartered
1½ cups diced yellow onion
3 tablespoons minced fresh garlic
2 tablespoons dry white wine or water
⅓ cup chopped fresh basil, or 3 tablespoons **Basil-garlic purée** (see page 82)
2 teaspoons red wine vinegar
¼ teaspoon red chile flakes

1. Preheat oven to 400°.
2. Partially peel eggplant: Remove ends. Working top to bottom, remove ¾-inch strips, creating a striped effect. Cut into 1-inch cubes.
3. Toss eggplant cubes in a large bowl with 1 teaspoon of the salt and ½ teaspoon of the pepper; set aside for 10 minutes. Toss cubes with 3 tablespoons of the oil and spread on a baking pan. Bake 20 minutes, or until browned and soft.
4. Toss zucchini with 2 tablespoons oil and ½ teaspoon each salt and pepper, and spread on a baking pan. Bake 20 to 25 minutes, or until lightly browned and soft, but not mushy.
5. Toss tomatoes with 1 tablespoon oil and ½ teaspoon each salt and pepper, and spread on a baking pan. Bake 15 minutes; set aside. When cool, remove skins from tomatoes.
6. Heat 2 tablespoons oil in a medium sauté pan over medium-high heat until it SHIMMERS. Add onion and sauté 3 to 5 minutes, until translucent. Remove from heat and stir in garlic and wine; cover and set aside for 10 minutes.
7. Combine all the roasted vegetables, the onion mixture, basil, vinegar, and chile flakes in a large bowl. Mix gently with a rubber spatula so as not to break up vegetables.

Notes:
   + The above method for roasting zucchini is useful for many vegetables, such as mushrooms, diced bell peppers, and poblano chiles. Cooking times may vary.
   + If you have three baking pans, the vegetables can all go into the oven at the same time. The cooking times vary, so remove each one after the cooking time specified above.
   + Serve roasted ratatouille at room temperature with chicken, pork, grilled meats, or your favorite vegetarian entrée.

Green salad with roasted beets,
Mezzo Secco cheese, and red pepper–sherry dressing

Roasted beets have a wonderfully concentrated flavor, and roasted peppers create a silky dressing. The nuttiness of Vella's award-winning cheese completes this richly flavored salad.

Serves 8

Roasted beets (recipe follows)
Red pepper–sherry dressing (recipe follows)
¾ pound mixed baby lettuces
¼ pound Vella Mezzo Secco cheese, shaved*

1. Make **Roasted beets** and **Red pepper–sherry dressing**.
2. Cut beets in half from stem to top, then into ⅛-inch slices.
3. Place lettuce in a large bowl and toss with just enough dressing to coat lightly. Arrange sliced beets around greens and place shaved cheese on top.

* Vella Mezzo Secco is a semi-firm cheese made in Sonoma. It can be ordered from the website or by telephone. Go to www.vellacheese.com or call 800-848-0505. Although the flavor is very different, a good imported Parmesan cheese (not pre-grated) can be substituted.

Roasted beets

2½ pounds beets (about 6 to 8 medium)
½ cup water

1. Preheat oven to 375°.
2. Trim ends from beets and rinse. If any beets are bigger than a plum, cut in half. Place beets and water in an 8-by-8-by-2-inch baking pan and cover tightly with foil.
3. Bake 1½ hours. Cool, still covered, 15 minutes. Discard any remaining water. Peel beets.

Note:
+ Roasted beet variations: chill and marinate in rice wine vinegar; combine with orange segments and orange zest. Or marinate beets in red wine vinegar, then combine with thinly sliced red onions, salt, and pepper. Serve beets hot with butter, purée and use for borscht, or use in **Chocolate beet cake**.

Red pepper–sherry dressing

Makes about 1¾ cups

1 **Roasted red pepper** (¾ cup packed) (page 203)
1 tablespoon minced fresh garlic
½ cup good sherry vinegar*
1½ teaspoons kosher salt
⅛ teaspoon cayenne pepper
¾ cup good olive oil

1. Place all ingredients except oil in a blender. Blend on high speed for 10 seconds, or until very smooth.
2. With the motor running, add oil in a thin stream until it is fully incorporated. (See EMULSIFY in Resources: Glossary.)

High-quality sherry vinegar is available in gourmet grocery stores. A good one is La Bodega, Vinagre de Jerez.

Raspberry pizza

Flat and thin-crusted, this easy dessert can be made with a variety of fruits, fresh or frozen. Here I've used raspberries, which are one of the highlights of summer in California. A light hand with the sugar allows the berries' natural tartness to come through, and orange zest adds a little perfume.

Serves 8/Makes 1 (10-inch) pizza

Cream cheese dough (recipe follows)
Raspberry filling (recipe follows)
¼ to ½ cup all-purpose flour for rolling out dough

1. Make **Cream cheese dough** and **Raspberry Filling.**
2. Preheat oven to 375°.
3. Place dough on a lightly floured work surface. Using as little flour as possible, roll out dough to a thickness of about ⅛ inch, forming a rough circle about 14 inches in diameter. Lightly oil a large cookie sheet or 12-inch pizza pan. Carefully transfer the dough circle to the pan. (Dough will hang over pan rim.)
4. Spread **Raspberry filling** to about 10 inches in diameter and ½-inch thick, leaving about 2½ inches of dough uncovered around the outside. Using a spatula or dough scraper to lift the dough, fold outside onto the filling in sections, working your way around the pizza. (The center of the pizza will remain exposed and the dough will look "pleated.") Pinch dough together to eliminate cracks.
5. Bake 35 to 40 minutes, until crust is brown and filling is bubbly around the outside. A little of the filling may leak out onto the baking sheet. Cool 20 minutes before cutting into wedges. Serve with whipped cream, ice cream, **Custard sauce**, **Raspberry sauce**, or any combination of these.

Cream cheese dough

Traditional pie dough recipes are full of dos and don'ts, such as cutting cold butter into flour and not overworking the dough. I think you'll find that my recipe is much less fussy and still yields a very tender crust.

Makes enough for one 10-inch pizza or pie

1 cup all-purpose flour
¼ teaspoon table salt
1 tablespoon sugar
¼ pound (1 stick) unsalted butter, softened
4 ounces cream cheese, softened

1. Sift flour, salt, and sugar together.
2. Add butter and cream cheese and mix by hand just until dough forms a ball. Do not overmix.

   Notes:
   + This dough may be frozen for up to a month. Flatten into a 6-inch disc and wrap twice with plastic wrap before freezing.
   + I often omit the sugar and use this dough for savory items such as mini empanadas (a turnover that can have any number of fillings, including black beans and cheese; ground beef or lamb, tomatoes, almonds, and raisins; and sausage and cheese) or hors d'oeuvre (pre-cook your favorite cased sausage, spread with a little Dijon-style mustard, and roll it up in dough; bake until lightly browned, and slice in ½-inch rounds).
   + I try to eliminate partially hydrogenated oils (such as white shortening) in my recipes. Here, cream cheese is a great replacement.
   + Cream cheese and butter can be softened together in the microwave. Try 10-second increments on high power.

Raspberry filling

18 ounces frozen or 3 (6-ounce) baskets fresh raspberries
¼ cup quick-cooking tapioca
½ cup sugar
2 teaspoons minced orange zest

1. Place fruit in a medium mixing bowl and toss gently with tapioca, sugar, and orange zest. Let sit for 15 minutes. Toss again before using.

   Notes:
   + Tapioca binds the filling and absorbs excess moisture. Any fruit can be used as a pie filling, but the tapioca amount may need to be adjusted. Fresh ripe peaches would work fine, but fresh figs aren't as juicy as raspberries and may not require any tapioca at all. Some experimentation will be required; the juicier the fruit, the more tapioca you should use.
   + Rinse whole oranges in hot water and dry them before zesting, to remove excess bitterness and any pesticide residue.

Eclectic Independence Day Dinner

On the Fourth of July, we celebrate freedom—the ideal that brought so many to our country. This menu celebrates the diversity for which California is famous. Bring on the fireworks!

Vietnamese spring rolls with tamarind dipping sauce

Teriyaki tri-tip steak

Wasabi mashed potatoes

Baby bok choy with sesame butter

Spinach salad with hearts of palm, oranges, and avocado dressing

Summer berry trifle with mango sauce

Vietnamese spring rolls
with tamarind dipping sauce

These fat-free little bundles, with fresh, crunchy vegetables and a hot-sweet-tart sauce, will have your guests double dipping.

Makes about 10 rolls

Tamarind dipping sauce (recipe follows)
1 (baseball-size) "nest" glass noodles*
½ cup grated carrot
½ cup grated English cucumber, squeezed to remove excess moisture
2 cups thinly sliced Napa cabbage
1 cup grated daikon radish or jicama, squeezed to remove excess moisture
¼ cup chopped green onion
¼ cup chopped fresh cilantro
¼ cup chopped fresh mint leaves
¼ cup chopped fresh basil leaves
10 Vietnamese spring roll wrappers (bánh tráng)*

1. Make **Tamarind dipping sauce**.
2. Cook noodles in a quart of boiling water until fully cooked, about 2 to 3 minutes; drain well. Cut noodles into 4-inch lengths.
3. Mix noodles, vegetables, and herbs together to make filling.
4. Arrange a work station: you'll need a clean cutting board or surface, a bowl of hot tap water, and a damp tea towel.
5. Lay the damp tea towel on the cutting board. Place 1 spring roll wrapper in the warm water. After 1 minute, carefully remove it and lay it on the tea towel. Place about ½ cup of filling on the bottom of the circle, spreading the filling to approximately 1 by 3 inches. Fold left and right sides of wrapper onto filling. Roll from bottom to top, gently pushing out the air as you go. The finished roll should be fairly tight.
6. Rolls are best eaten within a few hours, but they will keep 1 day, refrigerated. If serving (up to a day) later, place rolls on damp paper towels, seam side down; cover with more damp paper towels, then plastic wrap.
7. Cut rolls across the middle at an angle. Arrange rolls on a tray, cut side pointing up, with a small bowl of dipping sauce alongside.

   Notes:
   + When grating cucumbers, grate just down to the seeds, and continue grating and rotating until all that is left is the core. Discard this core so the filling will not be too juicy.
   + Rolling attractive, firm spring rolls that stay together when sliced takes a little practice. Try doubling this recipe if it's your first time, as there are bound to be a few mishaps.
   + For weddings and special parties I like to dress up these rolls by removing the petals from edible flowers (pansies, nasturtiums, chive blossoms) and sprinkling them on the upper portion of the wrap before rolling so they show through. Finely cut chives or black sesame seeds are pretty as well.

- If you have a Japanese mandolin (see Resources: Tools and Equipment), use it instead of a grater to shred the carrot, cucumber, and radish or jicama into long, thin strips. This will result in a more attractive, longer-lasting roll, as the Japanese mandolin makes cleaner cuts than a grater.
- Many ingredients can be incorporated into spring rolls; try cooked shrimp or ground pork, smoked chicken or duck, baked tofu or tempeh, sprouts, or spicy greens such as arugula, watercress, or dandelion greens.
- Use leftover noodles in Thai curries, in bowls of broth, or in cold noodle salads dressed with peanut sauce, or a mixture of fish sauce, lime juice, sambal oelek, and **Sweet-sour syrup** (see Essential Recipes).

Tamarind dipping sauce

Makes about ⅓ cup

¼ cup seasoned rice wine vinegar
2 teaspoons tamarind concentrate*
1 tablespoon sugar
1 teaspoon sambal oelek chili garlic sauce*
½ teaspoon fish sauce*
½ teaspoon minced fresh ginger
1 teaspoon minced fresh garlic
1 tablespoon water

1. Place all ingredients in blender, and blend for 2 seconds.

Available in Asian markets or the Asian foods section of some grocery stores; see Resources: Asian Ingredients for more information.

Teriyaki tri-tip steak

This teriyaki sauce imparts a deep, complex flavor and tenderizes an inexpensive cut of beef. Start this recipe the day before to allow time for the tri-tip to marinate overnight.

Serves 6 to 8

2 cups **Teriyaki sauce** (recipe follows)
2 pieces (about 3 pounds) tri-tip or flank steak

1. Make **Teriyaki sauce.**
2. Trim tri-tips of any excess fat or gristle. Place steaks in a medium bowl and cover with teriyaki sauce. Cover and refrigerate overnight.
3. Preheat oven to 350°.
4. Place steaks on a lightly oiled baking pan (discard sauce) and roast 15 minutes. Turn steaks over and roast another 5 to 15 minutes, depending on desired doneness: 20 minutes (total roasting time) will yield a very rare steak; 30 minutes, medium rare to medium. To be sure, check early with an instant meat thermometer inserted at the thickest part.
5. Let steaks rest for at least 15 minutes in a warm place before cutting. Cut across the grain in thin slices. Drizzle with a little more teriyaki sauce if desired.

> Notes:
> + Doneness guide:
>   Rare=110° to 115°
>   Medium-rare=120° to 125°
>   Medium=130° to 135°
>   Well-done=140° and above
>
>   These temperatures are based on my observations, and may seem a little low compared to other guides. Here's why: Meat temperatures will rise another 5 to 10 degrees after being removed from heat. Meat can always be cooked more, but it cannot be uncooked.
> + Marinated tri-tip can also be cooked on the grill. Let coals burn down slightly more than usual; due to the sugar in the sauce, steaks will burn if coals are too hot. Arrange steaks on one side of grill, not over hot coals. Cooking time on the grill will vary from oven directions above; if unsure, follow doneness guide.
> + Marinating overnight will make the steaks firmer, so testing doneness by "feel" is a little more difficult.
> + Teriyaki sauce darkens the color of the meat to a depth of about ⅛ inch.
> + This method produces a very flavorful steak; slice any leftovers thinly and serve with sushi rice or bowls of noodles in broth, on sandwiches, or simply fanned out on a platter with some sliced green onions on top.

Wasabi mashed potatoes

If you enjoy sushi, you'll like these "mashers," infused with just enough wasabi to clear the head.

Serves 6 to 8/Makes about 8 cups

8 large russet potatoes, peeled and cut into ½-inch chunks (about 3 pounds)
3 tablespoons wasabi powder
3 tablespoons water
¼ pound (1 stick) unsalted butter
1 tablespoon rice wine vinegar
1 cup plain yogurt
1 teaspoon kosher salt
¼ teaspoon white pepper

1. Bring 3 quarts water and 1 tablespoon salt to a boil in a large pot. Add potatoes and bring to a boil. Reduce heat and simmer 6 to 10 minutes, until potatoes start to fall apart.
2. While potatoes are boiling, make wasabe paste: mix wasabi powder and 3 tablespoons water until smooth, then set aside.
3. Drain potatoes well in colander, then place in a large mixing bowl. Add butter, vinegar, yogurt, kosher salt, pepper, and wasabe paste. Mash all together with potato masher, or whip with an electric mixer.

Notes:
+ Potatoes can be whipped in a stand mixer. This results in the smoothest potatoes. Potatoes should be very hot, and whipped just until smooth. If overwhipped, they become "gluey," due to their high starch content.
+ Other types of potatoes can be used, such as Yukon Golds, red or "new" potatoes, and even purple potatoes.

Baby bok choy with sesame butter

The mild flavor of bok choy is complemented by the garlic, green onion, and soy sauce in the flavored butter.

Serves 8

Sesame butter (recipe follows)
2 teaspoons kosher salt
6 baby bok choy (about 1¾ pounds)

1. Make **Sesame butter**.
2. Bring about 2 quarts water and the salt to a boil in a large saucepan or small stockpot.
3. Trim bok choy of any bad outer leaves and cut in half lengthwise. Wash in cold water.
4. Place bok choy in boiling water and blanch until tender, 3 to 5 minutes. Remove from water and drain well in colander. Blot excess water with paper towels or clean tea towels.
5. Place bok choy in a large mixing bowl, add sesame butter, and toss carefully. Arrange bok choy on a platter.

   Notes:
   + To make this recipe ahead of time: After draining in colander, spread bok choy on a baking pan and allow to cool completely. Blot excess water as directed above and arrange on a lightly oiled oven-safe platter. When almost ready to serve, place platter in preheated 350° oven for 5 minutes or until heated through. Place pats of sesame butter on top and serve.
   + Black sesame seeds (available in Asian markets) make a nice garnish.

Sesame butter

Makes about 1 cup

¼ pound (1 stick) unsalted butter, softened
2 tablespoons toasted sesame oil
1 tablespoon toasted sesame seeds
1 tablespoon rice wine vinegar
1 tablespoon minced fresh garlic
¼ cup chopped green onion
1 tablespoon soy sauce
1 scant teaspoon kosher salt

1. Combine all ingredients in a bowl and mix well. Cover and set aside until ready to use.

   Note:
   + Butter can also be rolled in plastic wrap to form logs. Label and store in the refrigerator for up to 1 week or in the freezer for up to 2 months. Try this COMPOUND BUTTER with white rice, or on baked or steamed fish.

Spinach salad
with hearts of palm, oranges, and avocado dressing

This salad is as healthful as it is beautiful. The avocado dressing contains no added oil, the spinach and citrus fruits are high in vitamins, and the hearts of palm contribute a tropical note.

Serves 8

Avocado dressing (recipe follows)
1 (14-ounce) can hearts of palm, drained
¾ pound baby spinach
2 oranges, peeled and cut into chunks
¼ cup chopped green onion

1. Make **Avocado dressing.**
2. Trim hearts of palm: look for discolored outer sections on the tube-like hearts. As with onions, outer layers can be fibrous and tough; remove and discard any tough layers. Slice hearts into ⅛-inch "coins."
3. Place baby spinach in a large bowl and toss with just enough dressing to lightly coat. Arrange orange chunks around spinach, and place hearts of palm and green onions on top.

Avocado dressing

This is one of my favorite dressings: silky smooth, full-bodied yet delicate, and a cinch to make.

Makes 1 cup

1 tablespoon lemon juice
3 tablespoons seasoned rice wine vinegar
½ cup ripe avocado (about ¾ of a Hass avocado)
1 teaspoon kosher salt
½ teaspoon minced fresh garlic
½ cup cold water
⅛ teaspoon white pepper
Small pinch of cayenne pepper

1. Place all ingredients in a blender. Blend on high speed for 5 seconds, until smooth.

   Notes:
   + This dressing is fairly thick and will thicken more as it sits. Thin with a little water if necessary.
   + I've found this dressing to be a good match with almost any type of greens.
   + This dressing provides a good way of using up leftover guacamole; substitute an equal amount of guacamole for the avocado. Taste before adding cayenne pepper.

Summer berry trifle
with mango sauce

Trifle is an English dessert that has many variations. The elements usually include sponge cake soaked with a sweet syrup, custard, fruit, and a fruit sauce. Here I've replaced the sponge cake with ladyfingers and lightened the custard with whipped cream, to make a more mousse-like dessert. Although trifle is traditionally served in a large clear bowl, I like to present it in wineglasses.

Serves 8

Pastry cream (recipe follows)
Rum syrup (recipe follows)
Mango sauce (recipe follows)
8 ladyfingers
1½ cups chopped fresh pineapple
1 (6-ounce) basket fresh raspberries (about 1 cup)
8 mint leaves

1. Make **Pastry cream**, **Rum syrup**, and **Mango sauce**.
2. Place 8 large wineglasses on a tray. Break up one ladyfinger cookie into each glass. Divide the syrup equally among the glasses. (It may seem like a lot of syrup, but the cookies will soak it all up.)
3. Divide the pastry cream among the glasses, using a soup spoon or a pastry bag so the pastry cream doesn't touch the sides of the glasses.
4. Divide pineapple and raspberries equally among the glasses, then add mango sauce.
5. Top with little dollops of the remaining pastry cream and garnish with mint leaves.

Pastry cream

This custard is a standard in the pastry chef's repertoire. It is used to fill éclairs, breakfast pastries, and cakes, often without the whipped cream.

Makes 2½ cups

1 cup whole or low-fat milk
1 tablespoon plus 2 teaspoons cornstarch
¼ cup plus 2 tablespoons sugar
Pinch of kosher salt
1 egg
1 teaspoon vanilla extract
½ cup whipping cream
1 tablespoon powdered sugar

1. Bring milk just to a boil in a heavy saucepan (preferably stainless steel).
2. Whisk cornstarch, sugar, salt, egg, and vanilla together in a mixing bowl. Pour in hot milk mixture, whisking constantly. Return mixture to the saucepan and cook over medium-high heat until custard bubbles, whisking constantly. Continue cooking as it boils for 3 to 5 seconds. The custard must boil briefly to thicken correctly and to cook out the raw cornstarch taste.
3. Place custard in a small bowl. Press plastic wrap onto the surface of the custard to prevent a skin from forming on top, and refrigerate at least 20 minutes.
4. Whip cream with powdered sugar to soft-peak stage, then fold into custard. Use immediately, or cover and refrigerate until ready to use.

> Notes:
> + When bringing milk to a boil, stir a few times—it's easy to burn the bottom.
> + If custard seems lumpy, whisk vigorously before folding in whipped cream. If lumps persist, process a few seconds until smooth in food processor fitted with blade before folding in whipped cream

Rum syrup

Makes 1½ cups

½ cup sugar
½ cup water
¼ cup white rum
¼ cup orange juice

1. Bring sugar and water to boil in a small saucepan. Remove from heat and cool. Add rum and orange juice.

Mango sauce

Makes 1 cup

¾ cups chopped fresh mango
¼ cup orange juice or water
2 teaspoons sugar

1. Place all ingredients in a blender and blend for 10 seconds, or until very smooth. Use immediately, or cover and refrigerate until ready to use.

> Notes:
> + This sauce will thicken slightly when stored; thin with water as needed.
> + This sauce is very colorful and rich. Make extra, store in zip-top bags, and freeze for up to a month. Use for elegant dessert presentations (pair with **Chocolate beet cake** or **Panna cotta**), salad dressings, smoothies, or cocktails such as mango Margaritas or Daiquiris.

Bastille Day Celebration

In 1789, the people of Paris rose up and stormed the state prison known as the Bastille. Overthrowing the ancient regime proved that the power belonged to the citizens and not to the king. Like our Fourth of July, this holiday is a celebration of liberty. For me, this holiday is a good occasion to create a French-inspired menu that is both classic and modern.

Salmon in a parchment "purse" with fennel and sun-dried tomato–black olive butter

Salt-roasted new potatoes

Asparagus with béaronnaise sauce

Arugula salad with heirloom tomatoes, pine nuts, and balsamic-honey vinaigrette

Chocolate mousse with raspberries and their sauce

Salmon in a parchment "purse"
with fennel and sun-dried tomato—black olive butter

This salmon presentation is a real crowd-pleaser. When the parchment purses are opened at the table, wonderful aromas billow up in an irresistible invitation to begin.

Serves 6

Sun-dried tomato—black olive butter (recipe follows)
2 bulbs fennel (sweet anise)
2 lemons, cut into ¼-inch slices
6 (6-ounce) salmon steaks, sliced from boneless fillets
Kosher salt
Black pepper
2 egg whites, slightly beaten with 1 tablespoon water
Kithcen twine

1. Make **Sun-dried tomato—black olive butter.**
2. Preheat oven to 350°.
3. Trim fennel bulbs, discarding tough outer parts, and cut into ⅛-inch slices. Boil a quart of water in a small saucepan and cook the fennel for about 20 seconds. Drain, then spread on a baking pan to cool. Divide cooled fennel and lemon rounds into 6 portions.
4. Cut 6 pieces of parchment paper into 12-inch rounds.
5. For each serving, lay a portion of fennel on the paper, then a piece of salmon. Sprinkle salmon lightly with salt and pepper. Top with a ¼-inch slice of the tomato-olive butter and a slice of lemon.
6. "Paint" the egg white mixture in a circle around the salmon, midway between the salmon and the edge of the parchment paper. Gather the parchment at the top and twist it, leaving as much airspace as possible above the salmon. Tie tightly with twine, making a bowknot. It should look like a "beggar's purse."
7. Bake 6 to 10 minutes, until paper is puffed and lightly browned. Do not overbake.
8. Place purses on plates. At the table, pass clean scissors, instructing guests to cut off the top, just below the twine.

> Notes:
> + This is a good preparation for halibut or any firm-fleshed white fish.
> + Aluminum foil can be used instead of parchment, but the presentation is not as elegant.

Sun-dried tomato–black olive butter

¼ cup pitted Kalamata olives
1 ounce sun-dried tomatoes (about 10 pieces)
¼ cup dry white wine
2 teaspoons balsamic vinegar
2 teaspoons minced fresh garlic
1 tablespoon tomato paste
2 teaspoons lemon juice
1 teaspoon kosher salt
½ teaspoon black pepper
½ pound (2 sticks) unsalted butter, softened

1. Rinse, drain, and chop olives roughly.
2. Heat tomatoes and wine in a small saucepan to a boil, reduce heat to lowest setting, and simmer 10 minutes, covered. Remove from heat and set aside to steam and soften tomatoes another 5 minutes. Cool and chop tomatoes roughly, saving any juice that remains.
3. Place tomatoes and their cooking liquid, olives, vinegar, garlic, tomato paste, lemon juice, salt, and pepper in food processor. Process until everything is chopped evenly but not puréed. Turn out into a bowl, add butter, and mix well. Roll mixture tightly in plastic wrap to form logs about the diameter of a silver dollar and refrigerate.

Note:
+ The extra butter can be frozen for up to a month.

Salt-roasted new potatoes

This dish is as comforting as it is simple. The salt seals in moisture as the potatoes bake, resulting in creamy, full-flavored potatoes that don't taste overly salty.

Serves 6 to 8

2 pounds baby red potatoes
2 teaspoons kosher salt

1. Preheat oven to 375°.
2. Wash and drain potatoes well. While still wet, toss potatoes with salt in a medium mixing bowl to coat. Place on a lightly oiled baking pan and roast for ½ hour, or until tender.

Notes:
+ Baking time may vary, depending on the size of the potatoes. It is important that the potatoes are left whole to seal in flavor. Choose potatoes that are about 1½ inches in diameter.
+ Small Yukon Gold potatoes are very flavorful and may be substituted for red potatoes.

Asparagus with béaronnaise sauce

Béarnaise is a tarragon-flavored butter and egg yolk sauce that is impressively rich. Some cooks find the recipe intimidating. My adaptation, "béaronnaise," utilizes the classic tarragon-vinegar reduction, combined with mayonnaise for richness.

Serves 6 to 8

1 tablespoon kosher salt
Béaronnaise sauce (recipe follows)
2 (1-pound) bunches asparagus, trimmed
About 2 cups ice cubes

1. In a large pot, bring salt and about 1 gallon water to a boil. Make **Béaronnaise sauce**.
2. Leaving rubber bands on bunches, place asparagus in boiling water and cook on high heat for 4 to 5 minutes, depending on the thickness of the stalks and your texture preference. Meanwhile, place about ½ gallon cold water and the ice cubes in a large bowl. When asparagus is cooked, immediately plunge it into the ice water to stop the cooking. When cool, remove stalks from water and drain well. Discard rubber band. Arrange stalks on a platter and drizzle with **Béaronnaise sauce**, or pass it separately.

Notes:
- Leave the rubber band on when cutting and cooking, to hold the asparagus together. (You may have to move the rubber band up a little toward the tips.)
- To trim asparagus: Remove one stalk and, holding it near the bottom with both hands, bend it until it breaks. The breaking point is usually where the stalk begins to change color and toughen. Cut the rest of the stalks at about this spot.
- Prepare the ice water as soon as you place the asparagus in the boiling water. When you think the asparagus is cooked, remove one stalk, plunge it into the ice water, and test it immediately for doneness.
- Asparagus lovers will surely have a preference as to the texture of cooked asparagus. I believe the range given above will please most palates.
- This dish can also be served warm. Simply omit the ice water procedure and serve asparagus immediately with the sauce.

continued⟶

Asparagus
with béaronnaise sauce

continued from previous page

Béaronnaise sauce

Makes about 1 cup

1 small shallot, peeled and minced
1 cup white wine vinegar
1½ tablespoons chopped fresh tarragon
1 cup good mayonnaise (such as Best Foods)
¾ teaspoon kosher salt

1. Make a reduction: Place shallot, vinegar, and tarragon in a small saucepan (preferably stainless steel). Bring to a boil over high heat and cook until liquid is reduced to about ¼ cup. Set aside to cool.
2. Stir 2 tablespoons of liquid into mayonnaise; add salt and stir again. Refrigerate extra liquid and use to flavor dressings or marinades.

Note:
+ This is a strongly flavored sauce. If you are really fond of the flavor of tarragon, try adding another teaspoon or so of chopped fresh tarragon at the end, with the salt.

Arugula salad with heirloom tomatoes, pine nuts, and balsamic-honey vinaigrette

Peppery arugula, spiced nuts, balsamic vinegar, and a bit of honey create a richly flavored backdrop for the real star of summer: heirloom tomatoes.

Serves 8

Spiced pine nuts (recipe follows)
Balsamic-honey vinaigrette (recipe follows)
¾ pound arugula, preferably small leaves
2 pounds heirloom tomatoes

1. Make **Spiced pine nuts** and **Balsamic-honey vinaigrette**.
2. Toss arugula with just enough dressing to coat lightly. Slice tomatoes and arrange around greens in a large bowl. Sprinkle with pine nuts.

Spiced pine nuts

Makes ½ cup

1 tablespoon brown sugar
1 teaspoon tamari soy sauce
1 teaspoon water
½ teaspoon granulated garlic
½ teaspoon kosher salt
¼ teaspoon black pepper
⅛ teaspoon cayenne pepper, or 1 teaspoon Tabasco sauce
½ cup pine nuts

1. Preheat oven to 350°. Mix all ingredients except nuts. Coat nuts with mixture and transfer to an oiled baking pan.
2. Bake 4 minutes, rotate pan front to back, and bake 3 minutes more. Transfer nuts onto a plate to cool.

continued——▶

Arugula salad with heirloom tomatoes, pine nuts, and balsamic-honey vinaigrette

continued from previous page

Balsamic-honey vinaigrette

Makes 1½ cups

¼ cup good balsamic vinegar
3 tablespoons warm honey
2 tablespoons lemon juice
1 tablespoon red wine vinegar
1 teaspoon kosher salt
½ teaspoon black pepper
2 tablespoons orange juice
1 cup canola oil

1. Place all ingredients except canola oil in a blender or food processor. With the motor running, add canola oil in a thin stream until all oil is incorporated. (See EMULSIFY in Resources: Glossary.)

   Notes:
   + Honey acts as the emulsifier (or thickening agent) in this dressing.
   + Warm honey in 10-second increments in the microwave so that it mixes in easily.

Chocolate mousse
with raspberries and their sauce

One day I was tinkering with a chocolate mousse recipe, looking for ways to lighten the texture. Most recipes include egg yolks and suggest adding melted chocolate directly to cold whipping cream, which often results in small lumps. Removing the egg yolks and melting the chocolate with a little cream creates a lighter, smoother mousse that has all the rich chocolate flavor one expects from this sublime dessert.

Serves 8

2 cups cold whipping cream, divided
½ pound good-quality bittersweet chocolate, finely chopped
3 egg whites
5 tablespoons sugar
1 pint fresh raspberries
1 cup **Raspberry sauce** (page 202)

1. Heat ½ cup cream just to a boil in a small saucepan. Remove from heat and add chocolate. Cover and let sit 5 minutes, then whisk until smooth.
2. Whip remaining 1½ cups cream to soft-peak stage. Set aside and keep cold.
3. Place eggs, uncracked and in their shells, in a bowl. Cover with hot tap water and let sit for about 5 minutes. Change hot water and let sit another 5 minutes. Separate eggs and discard yolks (or use for another recipe, such as **Custard sauce**). Make a meringue: In a medium mixing bowl, beat egg whites and sugar with an electric mixer to soft-peak stage (see Notes).
4. With a rubber spatula, fold chocolate mixture into egg whites, then fold in whipped cream. Do not overmix. Scoop mousse into 8 (6-ounce) ramekins or wine glasses. Cover with plastic wrap and refrigerate at least 2 hours, or up to 2 days.
5. Prepare **Raspberry sauce**. Top each serving of mousse with 2 tablespoons sauce and about 6 raspberries.

   Notes:
   + Due to variances in volume when cream and egg whites are whipped, this recipe may make an extra portion.
   + Make sure there are no specks of egg yolk in the whites before whipping.
   + Overwhipping cream or egg whites can result in a grainy mousse.
   + The French technique for making a meringue involves beating the egg whites and sugar over a flame. My technique of warming the eggs before separating them is much simpler.
   + The degree of risk associated with harmful bacteria in raw eggs can vary. Use only raw eggs purchased from a reliable source. For more information, see the American Egg Board website, www.aeb.org.
   + Purées made from tart fruits usually pair well with chocolate mousse: try cherry, blackberry, cranberry, or passion fruit. For a classic chocolate-vanilla pairing, match this mousse with **Custard sauce**.

Birthday Party at the Beach

We all know someone with a summertime birthday. Since nobody wants to work too hard at the beach, this menu has fewer recipes and most can be made ahead of time. Eating food hot off the grill is one of the enjoyable traditions of the beach, but the chicken can baked ahead and served cold.

Some hints for getting organized before you go:

+ Clean the oysters at home or bring a scrub brush to the beach. Pack an "oyster kit" with a shucking knife and a glove or old towels. Put the sauce in a squeeze bottle.
+ Marinate the chicken the night before, preferably in a plastic container with a cover. Pack a "grill kit" of tongs and a large mixing bowl.
+ Make the tomato and mozzarella platter ahead, and add the dressing at the beach.
+ Slice the cake into wedges before leaving home.

Oysters: the raw and the cooked

Rosemary-lemon chicken

Celery root and jicama salad with oranges and almonds

Tomato and fresh mozzarella platter with basil-garlic purée

Chocolate-almond cake

Oysters: the raw and the cooked

Oysters can evoke strong emotions. Purists argue that less is more, and perhaps they're right: few culinary experiences can compare to eating a freshly shucked oyster dressed with nothing more than a squeeze of lemon. However, I've found that oysters have an affinity for the sweet and the sour. Here are two ways to prepare them. Purchase three to four oysters per person.

Pacific rim mignonette (for raw oysters on the half shell)

Mignonette is a French sauce that contains red wine vinegar, shallots, and white pepper. This version was inspired by a delightful sauce I tasted at the Hog Island Oyster Company near Point Reyes National Seashore.

Makes 1 cup/Enough for 16 oysters

½ cup seasoned rice wine vinegar
¼ cup sake
2 tablespoons chopped cilantro
2 tablespoons lime juice
1 tablespoon minced jalapeño pepper
2 tablespoons minced shallot, red onion, or green onion

1. Mix ingredients well.
2. Shuck oysters, making sure to free each one from the bottom shell, or "cup." Leave oyster in bottom shell and top with a spoonful of sauce.

Ginger-lime butter (for grilled oysters)

This compound butter brings together the richness of butter and the bright flavors of ginger, lime, and jalapeño pepper.

Makes 1½ cups/Enough for 24 oysters

½ pound (2 sticks) unsalted butter, softened
2 teaspoons lime zest (from 1 lime)
3 tablespoons lime juice
2 tablespoons minced fresh ginger (from a walnut-size piece)
1 tablespoon minced jalapeño pepper
¾ teaspoon kosher salt
¼ teaspoon black pepper
1 tablespoon rice wine vinegar

1. Mix all ingredients well. Roll mixture in plastic wrap to form a 1-inch-diameter log. Refrigerate until firm.
2. Heat grill. Scrub and rinse oysters. Place oysters on a rack and grill over hot coals, covered, for about 5 minutes (depending on heat of grill). You may hear some of the oysters pop open. Remove oysters from grill with a pair of tongs and shuck, leaving oyster in the bottom shell, or "cup." Carefully pour off oyster "liqueur." Top each oyster with a slice of ginger-lime butter and return to the grill for 2 to 4 minutes, or until butter is melted and oyster is heated through. Do not overcook.

   Notes:
   + Shucking oysters: oysters are easy to shuck once they've cooked a bit. However, if you're confident shucking them raw, you can skip the initial grill time and pre-shuck instead. When shucking oysters, always use an oyster knife, wrap a towel around your left hand (or the hand holding the oyster), or wear a sturdy glove on that hand. Hold the oyster firmly on a stable surface while twisting the oyster knife into the "hinge" where the two shells come together. Once the knife is inside, sweep it around to free oyster from shell, then remove top shell. Sweep knife below the oyster to free it from bottom shell, or "cup," leaving oyster sitting in the cup. Remove any bits of shell from cup.
   + Oysters can be roasted in the oven instead of grilled. Bake in a preheated 400° oven 6 to 8 minutes.
   + A spoonful of **Chipotle barbecue sauce** is a terrific alternative to the gingery butter.

Rosemary-lemon chicken

Redolent of summer rosemary, this chicken can be baked or grilled, and served hot or cold. Salting the chicken twice seasons it inside and out. Be sure to marinate the chicken overnight, which flavors the bird right to the bone.

Serves 8

2 tablespoons minced fresh rosemary
1 tablespoon plus 1 teaspoon lemon zest (from 1 lemon)
2 tablespoons lemon juice (from 1 lemon)
¼ teaspoon dried red chile flakes
2 tablespoons minced fresh garlic
1 teaspoon sugar
¼ cup orange juice
2 tablespoons olive oil
1 teaspoon black pepper
2½ teaspoons kosher salt, divided
2 (3-pound) chickens, cut into 8 pieces each

1. In a small bowl, mix together all ingredients except chicken pieces and final teaspoon of salt.
2. Place chicken in a large mixing bowl and drizzle with rosemary-lemon mixture, coating well. Cover and refrigerate overnight.
3. Preheat oven to 375°.
4. Sprinkle chicken with 1 teaspoon kosher salt. Arrange chicken in a single layer on an oiled baking sheet and bake 15 to 20 minutes, or until chicken is cooked to the bone (juices will run clear when poked in thickest point with a knife tip).
5. Serve hot, or chill and serve up to two days later.

Celery root and jicama salad
with oranges and almonds

The combination of crunchy and chewy textures goes well with the creamy, tangy dressing in this simple salad.

Serves 8

Orange dressing (recipe follows)
4 cups celery root, peeled and cut into thin slivers
2 cups peeled jicama, cut into thin slivers
¾ cup chopped green onion
½ cup sliced almonds, toasted
Zest of 1 orange
2 oranges, peeled and separated into segments

1. Make **Orange dressing**.
2. Mix all salad ingredients except orange segments. Toss with dressing. Arrange orange segments around salad.

   Notes:
   + This salad will keep for one day, refrigerated.
   + The texture of this salad is best when the celery root and jicama are cut into thin slivers with a Japanese mandolin (see Resources: Tools and Equipment). If using a box grater, use the largest grater holes and try to get long strips.

Orange dressing

Makes 1½ cups

½ cup mayonnaise
½ cup low-fat plain yogurt
3 tablespoons cider vinegar
2 teaspoons kosher salt
3 tablespoons sugar
3 tablespoons orange juice concentrate

1. Whisk ingredients together until smooth.

Tomato and fresh mozzarella platter
with basil-garlic purée

This is a great example of what you can do with fresh ingredients and a simple preparation. The result is the essence of summer. If you can't get perfectly ripe tomatoes from a farmers market, good friends, or your own garden, substitute a different dish, such as roasted beets or steamed asparagus.

Serves 8

Basil-garlic purée (recipe follows)
2 pounds fresh heirloom, Early Girl, or Beefsteak tomatoes
1 (8-ounce) tub large fresh mozzarella balls
Kosher salt
Black pepper
2 tablespoons red wine vinegar

1. Make **Basil-garlic purée**.
2. Slice tomatoes and mozzarella balls into ¼-inch-thick rounds. Fan slices in layers on a platter, alternating tomatoes and mozzarella. Sprinkle with salt and freshly ground pepper. Drizzle with purée and vinegar.

   Notes:
   + Fresh mozzarella balls come packed in water and in different sizes. For this recipe I suggest the large egg-shaped "ovoline" mozzarella. Do not confuse this with blocks of mozzarella suited to grating for pizza.
   + In place of the red wine vinegar, try using **Balsamic vinegar reduction** (see Essential Recipes).

Basil-garlic purée

Like a smooth, simplified pesto, this purée preserves the basil in oil, retaining the leaves' intense bright-green color.

Makes ¾ cup

1½ cups basil leaves, roughly chopped (about 1 bunch)
¾ cup good olive oil
2 teaspoons minced fresh garlic
½ teaspoon kosher salt
2 teaspoons red wine vinegar

1. Place all ingredients in a blender. Blend on high speed 8 to 10 seconds, or until very smooth. Serve at room temperature, or cover and refrigerate for up to 6 days.

   Note:
   + I like to store purées and sauces in plastic squeeze bottles. Application is easier than with a spoon, and a squeeze bottle is useful for creating a striped effect.

Chocolate-almond cake

Soft, moist, and somewhat dense, this is a rich dessert with a strong scent of almond. Any extra cake goes nicely with a cup of tea.

Makes 1 (9-inch round) single-layer cake

¾ cup all-purpose flour
¾ cup cocoa powder
1 teaspoon baking powder
½ teaspoon baking soda
¼ teaspoon table salt
3 eggs
¼ pound (1 stick) unsalted butter
6 ounces almond paste*
2 tablespoons water
1¼ cups sugar
1¼ cups sour cream
1 teaspoon vanilla extract
Sweetened whipped cream (page 206)

1. Preheat oven to 350°.
2. Cut a circle of parchment paper to fit inside a 9-inch round cake pan. Lightly oil the pan, lay the parchment circle inside the pan, and lightly oil the paper.
3. Sift flour with cocoa powder, baking soda, and salt, and set aside.
4. Place eggs, uncracked and in their shells, in a bowl. Cover with hot tap water and let sit for about 10 minutes, then drain.
5. Place butter, almond paste, and water in a microwave-safe bowl and microwave for 30 to 45 seconds, or until butter is melted; place in a food processor bowl with eggs and sugar, and process 20 to 30 seconds, until very smooth. Add sour cream and vanilla and process just until combined. Turn mixture into a bowl and fold in flour mixture.
6. Pour batter into prepared cake pan (pan will seem very full, but this cake doesn't rise much) and bake 40 to 45 minutes, or until the center springs back when touched lightly and a skewer inserted in the middle comes out dry.
7. Cool 30 minutes in pan; run a paring knife around edge of pan, and turn out onto a rack to finish cooling.
8. Make **Sweetened whipped cream.**
9. Cut cake into wedges and serve with whipped cream.

Almond paste—not the same as marzipan—is available in the baking section of most supermarkets. Odense makes a good brand that comes in 7-ounce logs.

Fall Menus

Harvest Festival

Day of the Dead Dinner

Beaujolais Nouveau Fête

Virgin of Guadalupe Fiesta

Harvest Festival

From Latin, *equinox* is roughly translated as "equal night," so named because the day and night are the same length. The full moon closest to the fall equinox is known as the harvest moon, because crops are sometimes harvested by the bright lunar light. Bitter greens and comforting polenta in this menu reflect a shift toward the colder months.

Roasted pork loin with fennel-pepper crust and salsa verde

Soft polenta with Asiago cheese

Braised chard with browned garlic

Green salad with fennel, papaya, and blue cheese "snow"

Focaccia bread

Vanilla panna cotta with raspberry sauce

Almond-anise biscotti

Roasted pork loin
with fennel-pepper crust and salsa verde

This rustic dish is fragrant with fresh herbs and contrasting flavors. Brining the pork loin overnight makes it really juicy. Although this recipe takes some advance preparation, the results are well worth it.

Serves 6 to 8

2½ cups water
¼ cup lightly packed brown sugar, lightly packed
¼ cup kosher salt
1 tray ice cubes
3 pounds boneless pork loin

1. Bring water, brown sugar, and salt to a boil in a saucepan, then remove from heat. Pour brine into a 2-quart (or larger) container and add just enough ice cubes to measure 1 quart. Stir to dissolve ice.
2. Place loin in brine and refrigerate overnight. If loin is less than 4 inches in diameter, brine and refrigerate only 4 hours.
3. Preheat oven to 325°.
4. Remove pork loin from brine, wipe it dry with a paper towel, and lightly coat it with **Fennel-pepper crust**. Place loin on a roasting pan and roast 22 minutes, or until internal temperature is 145° at the thickest part (check with an instant-read thermometer, if you have one). Let rest 15 minutes in a warm spot.
5. Cut roast into ½-inch slices. Serve with **Salsa verde** on the side.

> Notes:
> + For more on brine and its uses, see **All-purpose brine** in Essential Recipes.
> + For this recipe, use center-cut pork loin—not tenderloin, which is smaller and more expensive. The darker meat at the end of the loin is the juiciest and most tender. Ask your butcher for it.

Fennel-pepper crust

2½ tablespoons whole fennel seeds
1 tablespoon plus 1 teaspoon whole black peppercorns

1. Grind spices together coarsely in an electric spice or coffee mill. Do not grind too long; seeds should be just broken up and mixture should have the texture of coarse sand.

Salsa verde

Basil and olive oil are a classic combination—but mint, sugar, and vinegar? Once you've tried this sauce, I bet you'll be looking for other dishes to serve it with.

Makes 1½ cups

½ cup chopped fresh basil leaves
1¼ cups chopped fresh Italian parsley
⅓ cup chopped fresh mint
¼ cup roughly chopped green onions
¼ cup roughly chopped red onion
2 teaspoons minced fresh garlic
½ cup good olive oil
1 teaspoon kosher salt
1 teaspoon sugar
½ cup dry white bread crumbs
3 tablespoons red wine vinegar

1. Place all ingredients in a food processor and process 4 or 5 seconds, or until smooth.

   Notes:
   + Try salsa verde with fresh tomatoes, grilled chicken breasts, grilled lamb, roast beef, or sliced bread. Or add a spoonful to vegetable soup.
   + A sharp food-processor blade is important for this recipe. A dull blade will only bruise the ingredients. Use a steel or hand-held knife sharpener to maintain the blade.

Soft polenta with Asiago cheese

Easy, versatile, comforting—polenta is truly a food for all seasons.

Serves 6 to 8

2 cups whole or low-fat milk
2 cups water or stock
⅓ cup minced yellow onion
1 teaspoon minced fresh garlic
¾ cup polenta
3 tablespoons unsalted butter
¼ cup freshly grated Asiago cheese
¾ teaspoon kosher salt

1. Bring milk, water, onion, and garlic to a boil in a heavy saucepan, then pour in polenta while whisking rapidly. Reduce heat to low and simmer, whisking frequently, for about 5 minutes.
2. Remove from heat and stir in butter, cheese, and salt. Serve immediately, or cover and keep warm for up to 30 minutes before serving.

Notes:
+ For a reduced-fat version, omit butter and add another ¼ cup water; and omit cheese and add another ¼ teaspoon salt.
+ Imported Parmesan cheese may be substituted for Asiago, but it is much more expensive.
+ If polenta seems too firm, whisk in a little water.
+ For soft polenta, use a 5-to-1 ratio, or 5 parts liquid of choice to 1 part polenta. For firm polenta (that can be chilled and cut into shapes), use a 4-to-1 ratio, or 4 parts liquid of choice to 1 part polenta.
+ There are many ways to serve polenta: mix or top with roasted poblano chiles (whole or puréed), bell peppers, dried chile purée, marinara, or basil pesto; for "lasagne," layer with grilled vegetables and cheese, and bake; for a GRATIN, cut into shapes, "shingle" in an oiled baking pan, top with cheese sauce, and bake; cut into shapes, brush with olive oil, and grill; or for a finger food, cut into little rounds, scoop a depression out of the top with a melon baller, fill with ingredients of choice, and bake.
+ Leftover polenta can be microwaved with a little liquid; or to return it to a creamy consistency, chop it, then heat slowly while whisking with some liquid.

Braised chard with browned garlic

Chard is winter soul food, and this is an easy, satisfying way to prepare it. The browned-garlic method is borrowed from Chinese wok cookery. Think hot, fast, and flavorful.

Serves 6 to 8

2 tablespoons olive oil
2 tablespoons minced fresh garlic
¼ cup dry white wine or water
3 bunches red, green, or rainbow chard, stemmed and roughly chopped (about 8 cups, packed)
½ teaspoon kosher salt
¼ teaspoon black pepper

1. Place all ingredients next to the stove.
2. In a large sauté pan over high heat, heat oil until it SHIMMERS, then add garlic. Stir and scrape pan with a spatula, watching carefully to avoid overcooking. How brown you cook the garlic determines the flavor of the finished dish: beige equals light flavor, dark brown equals toasty flavor.
3. After browning garlic, add wine, then add chard, salt, and pepper. Cook and stir on high heat until chard is fully wilted and soft, about 2 minutes.

   Notes:
   + After stemming and chopping chard, clean it by placing it in a bowl, adding water, and swishing it vigorously with your hand. Drain in a colander.
   + You may have to cook this recipe in two batches, depending on the size of your sauté pan. If your pan is less than 12 inches in diameter, make the garlic-wine mixture first and scrape it out into a small bowl. Rinse out the pan and cook chard in two batches, then toss them together with the garlic-wine mixture.
   + Try this variation: wilt the chard in a little olive oil, season with salt and pepper, and stir in about ¾ cup of **Caramelized onions** (see Essential Recipes).

Green Salad
with fennel, papaya, and blue cheese "snow"

This combination of flavors may seem odd, but this salad tastes like more than the sum of its parts. If you can't find all the ingredients, don't worry—the cheese, greens, and dressing are the essentials. Remember to freeze the cheese ahead of time, because the way it lightly coats the greens when grated over the salad is what makes this dish unique.

Serves 6 to 8

6-ounce piece of blue cheese
Lemon dressing (recipe follows)
¼ pound mixed salad greens
¼ pound arugula
1 medium papaya, peeled and diced
1 small jicama, peeled and cut into "matchsticks"

1. Place blue cheese in freezer for several hours or until frozen.
2. Make **Lemon dressing**.
3. Toss greens lightly with dressing, then place a handful of dressed greens on each plate. Arrange papaya and jicama around greens.
4. Using a grater with large holes, grate some of the cheese over each salad. Serve immediately.

   Notes:
   + If papaya is difficult to find, substitute two ripe pears or apples.
   + Small arugula leaves are more mild and tender than large ones.

Lemon dressing

Very light and tart, this dressing enhances the other salad ingredients without stealing the show. Use it for any salad that is going to be served with rich dishes.

Makes about ½ cup

2 tablespoons lemon juice
2 tablespoons balsamic vinegar
½ teaspoon kosher salt
¼ teaspoon black pepper
4 tablespoons good olive oil

1. Combine all ingredients in a jar with a tight-fitting lid and shake until well mixed.

Focaccia bread

Focaccia is the basis of most sandwiches in Italy. It is supposed to be a fast bread, but I've found that using a starter gives it more flavor. If you're short on time, omit the starter and increase the amounts of both water and flour by ½ cup.

Makes one 17-by-11-inch flat bread

1 cup **Sourdough starter** (recipe follows), cold from refrigerator
2 cups hot (120° to 130°) water
1 tablespoon sugar
2 teaspoons kosher salt
1 envelope (2¼ teaspoons) active dry yeast
4½ cups bread flour or all-purpose flour, preferably unbleached organic
¼ cup olive oil, plus extra for oiling dough and baking pan

1. Combine **Sourdough starter**, hot water, sugar, and salt in a large bowl. Mix in yeast and let sit 5 to 10 minutes.
2. Add 3 cups of the flour and beat with a wooden spoon for 1 minute. Add remaining flour and mix with a wooden spoon until dough is very stiff, then knead for 1 minute with lightly floured hands. Dough should be slightly moist.
3. Form dough into a ball and place in a large, oiled bowl. Lightly oil top of dough, cover bowl with plastic wrap, and let dough rise in a warm place 45 minutes to 1 hour.
4. Lightly oil an 17-by-11-by-1-inch baking pan. Place dough in pan and push it out until it touches the sides. "Dimple" dough lightly with fingertips and spread the ¼ cup of oil onto surface. Cover with plastic wrap or an inverted baking pan of the same size and let rise in a warm place for 30 to 45 minutes.
5. Preheat oven to 450°.
6. Bake bread 10 minutes, then turn the pan around, front to back, to ensure even browning. Bake 10 minutes more or until light brown all over. Remove from oven and slide focaccia onto cooling rack. Cool 10 minutes before cutting into squares.

Sourdough starter

Makes 3 cups

Tiny pinch of active dry yeast (about 10 grains)
1½ cups cold water
1½ cups organic whole wheat flour, bread flour, or all-purpose flour

1. Whisk all ingredients together briskly.
2. Store in a glass or plastic jar, and cover loosely so gas can escape.
3. Leave out at room temperature overnight to develop flavor and multiply yeasts. Refrigerate after that.

continued——>

Focaccia bread

continued from previous page

Notes:

- Rising time varies with the room temperature: warmer room equals faster rising. Slower rising develops more flavor. About 80° is ideal, but anywhere between 70° and 90° is fine.

- This recipe will fit in almost any baking pan(s) you have. If you have two smaller pans, divide the dough between them. If you have a flat cookie sheet with no rim, just spread out the dough roughly to the dimensions specified above. If you have a commercial bun pan or "half sheet pan" (13 by 18 inches), the dough will stretch out to fill that as well.

- To make crostini from focaccia, spread dough a little thinner than usual (about ½ inch) in the baking pan. When baked and cooled, cut focaccia in half horizontally, then into small triangles or squares. Toast lightly in the oven before topping with **Braised-garlic cream** and **Red pepper–olive spread**, or a spread of your choice.

- This is a very versatile dough. It can be pulled into rough shapes like ciabatta, used for calzone or pizza dough, or topped with any number of things: thinly sliced tomatoes, olives, caramelized onions, roasted vegetables, mixed seeds (try sesame, poppy, fennel, or a blend), salt, pepper, oil, or minced fresh garlic (cover with an upside-down baking pan for the first 10 minutes of baking time and uncover for the last 10 minutes to keep garlic from burning). Fill or roll with your favorite ingredients.

Vanilla panna cotta
with raspberry sauce

With a texture somewhere between flan and pudding, this is a delicious finale to any meal.
I serve this dish year-round with seasonal fruits. Panna cotta means "cooked cream" in Italian.

Serves 8

1 (¼-ounce) envelope unflavored gelatin (2½ teaspoons)
¾ cup whole or low-fat milk
¾ cup sugar
Pinch of kosher salt
1 cup sour cream or plain yogurt
1½ cups cold whipping cream
1 tablespoon vanilla extract
Raspberry sauce (page 202)

1. Sprinkle gelatin over milk in a small saucepan. Let sit 5 minutes to soften gelatin.
2. Add sugar and salt to gelatin-milk mixture, then whisk together. Bring almost to a boil (do not let boil) on medium heat, whisking often. Gelatin should be completely dissolved. Pour into a mixing bowl and set aside.
3. Whisk sour cream into gelatin-milk mixture until completely smooth. Whisk in cream and vanilla, just until everything is combined.
4. Pour mixture into eight 6-ounce ramekins or custard cups. Leave ¼ inch of headroom. (You may have a little of the mixture left over.) Tap each ramekin gently on a work surface to remove any bubbles. Cover and chill 4 hours or overnight before serving with **Raspberry sauce**.

Notes:
  + Panna cotta is a little like soft Jell-O: it can be poured into almost any mold, chilled, and served that way or turned out for a more elegant presentation. Even disposable plastic cups can be used as molds (do not fill molds more than 3 inches deep, or panna cotta will bulge or collapse when unmolded). Panna cotta can also be poured into a metal loaf pan or muffin tins; when chilled, dip pan into hot water just until panna cotta is soft around the edges, then turn out and arrange individual portions on plates. If you use a loaf pan, you'll have a fragile, loaf-shaped block, which must be cut into squares or triangles before plating. Make sure the panna cotta is very cold before unmolding, and wipe your knife with a hot, wet towel between cuts to make clean slices.
  + To make buttermilk panna cotta, substitute buttermilk for milk and add 1 teaspoon lemon juice. Make sure not to boil the mixture. This tart variation is perfect for serving with a sweet sauce, such as caramel.
  + To make black-bottom panna cotta, freeze **Chocolate mousse**, then cut into small cubes. Place a few cubes in the bottom of ramekins, pour panna cotta mixture over cubes, cover, and chill.
  + This dessert is great with almost any tart fruit or fruit purée: try plum, any kind of berry, passion fruit, or sour cherry.

Almond-anise biscotti

These classic super-crispy, twice-baked cookies go perfectly with ice cream, mousse desserts, and coffee, tea, or dessert wine. Maida Heatter's cookbooks inspired this recipe years ago.

Makes about 55 biscotti

2 eggs
¾ cup sugar
6 ounces (1½ sticks) unsalted butter, softened
1 teaspoon vanilla extract
¼ teaspoon almond extract (optional)
1½ cups all-purpose flour
2 teaspoons baking powder
1 cup whole almonds
1½ teaspoons anise seeds

1. Preheat oven to 325°. Place eggs, uncracked and in their shells, in a bowl. Cover with hot tap water and let sit for about 10 minutes.
2. Cream together sugar, butter, vanilla, and almond extract, if desired, with an electric mixer. Add one egg, mix on medium speed until incorporated, then add the other egg and mix.
3. Sift flour and baking powder together, then add to sugar-butter mixture. Add almonds and anise seeds, and mix with a wooden spoon just until combined.
4. Flour your hands and sprinkle some flour on the counter. Roll dough into 1-inch-diameter logs. Place logs on an oiled and floured (or parchment paper–lined) baking pan.
5. Bake 20 minutes, then turn pan, front to back, to ensure even browning. Bake 10 minutes more, until medium brown and firm throughout. As logs bake, they will sag and resemble giant cookies.
6. Remove from oven and cool 15 minutes. Reduce oven temperature to 250°.
7. Slide giant cookies onto a cutting board and cut diagonally into ⅝-inch slices with a sharp serrated bread knife. Place slices on same pan and bake another 10 minutes.
8. Flip cookies over and bake a final 10 minutes. Biscotti should be light brown and very crispy.

   Notes:
   + Almond extract enhances almond flavor when used sparingly but tastes artificial if overdone. The amount called for in this recipe is minimal.
   + Biscotti can be cut from ½ to ¾ inch thick, but they work best on the thick side because whole almonds tend to tear the cookie apart. Although sliced almonds will work in this recipe, I prefer the look and texture of whole almonds.
   + If you have a rack that fits in your baking pan, bake biscotti slices directly on the rack and you won't have to flip them at the last step.
   + Cooked biscotti may be dipped halfway in, or drizzled with, chocolate. I prefer bittersweet.
   + You'll be surprised how fast these cookies get eaten, but you can freeze a portion of the giant cookie, then slice and bake it later.

Day of the Dead Dinner

NOVEMBER 2

Day of the Dead is a unique Mexican holiday, blending sadness and festivity. It is a day to remember departed loved ones, but also to affirm life. Besides a good meal, Day of the Dead celebrations often involve a ceremony, with photographs, poems, votive candles, decorated sugar skulls and skeletons, and an abundance of marigolds.

Pork chili verde

Mexican rice

Smoky pinto beans

Chayote with jalapeño-lime dressing

Southwestern Caesar salad

Sponge cake with coconut custard

Pork chili verde

This stew-like dish is so tasty, I guarantee you'll be sopping up the last of the sauce with the tortillas.

Serves 6 to 8/Makes about 8 cups

3 pounds pork stew meat (pork butt), cut into 1-inch cubes
1 tablespoon kosher salt
1 teaspoon black pepper
2 large poblano chiles, seeded and roughly chopped
1 small white or yellow onion, roughly chopped
6 cloves garlic
1 (1-pound, 10-ounce) can whole tomatillos, drained (discard juice)
1 cup water
¾ cup roughly chopped cilantro
1 jalapeño pepper, roughly chopped (optional)
¼ cup canola or salad oil
12 to 16 flour tortillas

1. Roll pork in salt and pepper. Let sit 10 to 20 minutes.
2. Blend chiles, onion, garlic, tomatillos, water, cilantro, and jalapeño in blender for 15 to 20 seconds, until very smooth.
3. Heat a heavy saucepan over high heat until very hot. Add oil to pan, then pork. Sear pork on all sides until browned. Drain and discard oil. Return pork to the same pan and pour blended sauce over meat. Bring to a boil, reduce heat, and simmer, covered, about 1 hour. The meat should be very tender but not falling apart. If sauce seems thin, uncover and simmer another 5 to 10 minutes to thicken.
4. Warm flour tortillas in oven or on griddle and serve with the chili verde.

   Notes:
   + If you prefer mild dishes, omit the jalapeño.
   + Use both the leaves and stems of cilantro. The stems blend into the sauce.
   + You can buy pork butt (shoulder) and cut it into cubes yourself, or just buy pork stew meat cubes. Either way, check over the cubes and remove excess fat before cooking.

Mexican rice

The Latina cooks in our kitchen make perfect rice without measuring a thing. They toss tomatoes, onions, garlic, and water into a blender, then add the mixture to hot grains. I wrote down the amounts and their method so I could share them with you.

Serves 6 to 8/Makes about 4½ cups

2 tablespoons canola or salad oil
1½ cups jasmine or long-grain white rice
1½ cups water
1 (8-ounce) can tomato sauce
½ small yellow onion, finely diced
1 teaspoon minced fresh garlic
2 teaspoons kosher salt

1. In a medium saucepan, heat oil until it SHIMMERS. Add rice and cook, stirring, 5 to 8 minutes, until grains are lightly browned.
2. Add water, tomato sauce, onion, garlic, and salt. Stir together and bring to a boil. Reduce heat and simmer, covered, 15 minutes.
3. Remove from heat and let sit, covered, 5 minutes. Fluff with a fork.

Notes:
+ Mexican rice is typically made with long-grain white rice, but I prefer jasmine because of its rich flavor.
+ Toasting the rice is an important step that adds flavor and makes rice fluffy.
+ Add 1 small, diced fresh carrot to saucepan with rice, and/or add ¾ cup fresh or frozen peas a few minutes before fluffing, for color and texture.
+ If using a rice cooker, just place everything in the cooker, mix well, and follow the manufacturer's directions. Always use cold water to start.
+ Here is a simple formula for making most types of white rice: One cup dry rice will feed 4 to 5 as a side dish. Water should be 1½ times the rice volume; for example, for 4 servings as a side dish, cook 1 cup rice in 1½ cups water.
+ Brown rice takes longer to cook than white rice and needs slightly more water—cook 1 cup of brown rice in 1¾ cups of water, covered, for ½ hour.
+ For wild rice, use about 3 times as much water as rice. Simmer, uncovered, until tender (usually about 45 minutes) and drain in a colander.

Smoky pinto beans

I prefer whole pinto beans like these to the refried version. Often called soup beans, they can be used for filling burritos or quesadillas, or served with your favorite Mexican dish.

Serves 6 to 8/Makes about 3 cups

1½ cups dried pinto beans
1 quart hot tap water
1 tablespoon **Chipotle purée** (page 197)
1 teaspoon kosher salt

1. Pick through beans and discard any pebbles or dirt; rinse beans. Place beans and hot water in a saucepan and bring to a boil. Cover, reduce heat to low, and simmer 1 hour, or until beans are soft, stirring occasionally.
2. Make **Chipotle purée**. Stir 1 tablespoon purée into beans, add salt, and heat through.

   Notes:
   + If you soak beans overnight in cold water, they will cook a bit faster. Discard soaking water before cooking.
   + Cooked beans last no more than a few days in the refrigerator, but they freeze well.
   + Try black beans or small red beans with this recipe.

Chayote with jalapeño-lime dressing

Chayote is delicious, versatile, and readily available, yet unfamiliar to many people. Cooked chayote is juicy and firm like a honeydew melon, and tastes a bit like zucchini.

Serves 6 to 8

5 chayotes
2 quarts water
2 teaspoons kosher salt
Jalapeño-lime dressing (recipe follows)

1. Peel chayotes and cut into large cubes, including the seed.
2. Bring water and salt to a boil, add chayote cubes, and simmer 8 to 9 minutes, or until slightly firm but easy to cut with a knife. Drain and spread out on a baking pan to cool.
3. While chayote is cooling, make **Jalapeño-lime dressing.**
4. Transfer chayote to a bowl and toss with the dressing. Cover bowl with plastic wrap and marinate at room temperature 1 or 2 hours. Toss occasionally to coat chayote well with dressing.
5. Serve at room temperature.

Jalapeño-lime dressing

1 jalapeño pepper, seeded and minced
2 teaspoons roughly chopped cilantro
1 teaspoon minced fresh garlic
1 teaspoon kosher salt
Juice of 3 limes (about ⅓ cup)
⅓ cup olive oil

1. Whisk all ingredients together in a small bowl.

    Notes:
    + I used to discard the seed in the center of the chayote. When I discovered its nut-like flavor, I started cooking with it.
    + Chayotes can be peeled with a vegetable peeler, but you may need a paring knife to remove the deeply wrinkled skin.
    + Raw, peeled chayote has an unusual, slippery texture. Be careful when peeling and cutting—it can get away from you! Wash your hands well after handling chayote, or the sticky residue may cling to your skin. To peel large amounts, wear rubber gloves.
    + Jalapeño peppers vary considerably in spiciness. If you like hot foods, use the seeds. Wash your hands right after cutting jalapeños. Wear rubber gloves when handling large quantities.
    + If you're a real "chilehead," use 2 jalapeño peppers in this recipe.

Southwestern Caesar salad

The original Caesar salad was created in Tijuana, Mexico. The cumin, jalapeño, and lime in this recipe give the classic a Southwestern spin.

Serves 6 to 8

1¼ cups **Southwestern Caesar dressing** (recipe follows)
¼ cup **Tamari-roasted pumpkinseeds** (page 208)
2 grapefruits or oranges, peeled, seeded, and cut into sections
2 heads romaine lettuce
2 handfuls tortilla chips, broken into large pieces, divided

1. Make **Southwestern Caesar dressing** and **Tamari-roasted pumpkinseeds.**
2. Wash lettuce and slice into roughly rectangular pieces. For each serving, set aside two grapefruit sections for garnish.
3. Combine lettuce, half of chips, and remaining grapefruit with enough dressing to coat lettuce well. Place salad in a serving bowl, arrange the reserved grapefruit sections around edges, and top with remaining tortilla chips.
4. Sprinkle with the pumpkinseeds.

Notes:
+ If you don't have time to make your own **Tamari-roasted pumpkinseeds**, they can usually be found at natural foods stores.
+ Thinly sliced red onion can be added to this salad.

Southwestern Caesar dressing
This recipe makes more than enough dressing for the recipe above.

Makes 2¼ cups

¼ cup water
1 tablespoon red wine vinegar
4 cloves garlic
½ teaspoon black pepper
⅓ cup freshly grated Parmesan or Asiago cheese
1 egg
⅓ cup **Tamari-roasted pumpkinseeds** (page 208)
1 teaspoon ground cumin
2 teaspoons soy sauce
Juice of 3 limes (about ⅓ cup)
1½ teaspoons kosher salt
½ jalapeño pepper with seeds or ⅛ teaspoon cayenne pepper
1¼ cups canola or salad oil

1. Place all ingredients except oil in a blender. Blend on high speed until smooth, about 30 seconds.
2. With the motor running, add oil in a thin stream until it is fully incorporated. (See EMULSIFY in Resources: Glossary.) Dressing should have a creamy texture.

Notes:
+ If using lemon juice instead of lime, increase quantity to ½ cup.
+ Garlic lovers may want an extra clove in the salad dressing.
+ The degree of risk associated with harmful bacteria in raw eggs can vary. Use only raw eggs purchased from a reliable source. For more information, see the American Egg Board website, www.aeb.org.

To the Westerbeke cooks and food

Oh, chefs, how we love you!
You are the mansion that I visit in my dreams

Focaccia! Butternut squash!
Marzipan, tomatoes, heirloom, organic, beneath a festoon
Of papel picado, crepe-paper lilies
In all pastels, all
Is heaven-on-earthly
Each dish is a well-orchestrated ode
Sublime sensual stimulation
Figs and marzipan—
Caramel and brandied.
Yahoo!

I wait with the breath
of a hungry cougar
for the next moment I can leap upon
the tasty morsels of life.

Excerpt from poem by
California Poets in the Schools
October 12, 2003

Sponge cake with coconut custard

Moist cakes are a bit of an obsession with me, and they're always popular with our guests. After a number of experiments with a sponge cake recipe, I discovered what seems obvious now—adding a little water makes a moister cake. Combined with the creamy coconut custard, this is an unforgettable flavor-texture combination.

Makes 1 (9-inch round) cake

Coconut custard (recipe follows)
8 eggs
1⅓ cups sugar, divided
3 tablespoons canola oil
3 tablespoons water
2 teaspoons vanilla extract
1 cup all-purpose flour, sifted
¼ cup toasted coconut (from **Coconut custard** recipe)

1. Make **Coconut custard.**
2. Preheat oven to 350°. Oil and flour one 9-inch round cake pan.
3. Place eggs, uncracked and in their shells, in a bowl. Cover with hot tap water and let sit for about 10 minutes.
4. Remove eggs from water. Crack and separate eggs, putting yolks in a large glass or stainless steel bowl. With an electric mixer or a whisk, beat egg yolks with ⅓ cup of the sugar until pale and thick, about 4 to 6 minutes.
5. Wash and dry beaters or whisk. Whip egg whites with remaining 1 cup sugar until stiff but not dry. Whisk vanilla into yolks. Fold whites into egg yolks with a rubber spatula. Add oil and water to bowl. Immediately fold in flour in two additions. Do not overmix.
6. Pour batter into prepared pan and, with a knife or rubber spatula, spread batter so it is level. Bake 20 to 24 minutes. Do not overbake. When done, the cake will be golden brown and slightly domed, and will spring back when touched lightly in the middle.
7. Cool cake completely. Cake will fall a bit as it cools. Using a paring knife, carefully cut cake free from pan sides, then turn out and cut in half horizontally with a serrated knife.
8. To assemble cake: Keep the cake upside down so that the bottom, which is flatter, will become the top. Spread about half of coconut custard on the bottom layer. Place the other layer on top of filling. Use remaining custard to "frost" top and sides, then sprinkle reserved toasted coconut on top of cake.
9. Chill for at least 30 minutes. Cut into wedges to serve.

Notes:
- When you separate the eggs, make sure there is no yolk in the whites. Egg whites will not whip properly with any yolk in them.
- This recipe can also be baked in jelly roll pans. For sheet cakes, spread the batter ½- to ¾-inch thick in a prepared pan, but bake only 6 to 10 minutes. Do not overbake.
- Sheet cakes can be layered in a frozen ice cream cake, filled (with whipped cream, chocolate mousse, or custard) and rolled to make ROULADES, cut into cubes to make **Summer berry trifle**, or used for tiramisu.

Coconut custard

Pastry cream is a thick custard used in all sorts of breakfast pastries and desserts. Here, I've modified a pastry cream recipe to give it the maximum coconut flavor.

Makes 2½ cups

¾ cup unsweetened shredded coconut
½ cup whole, skim, or low-fat milk
1 (13½-ounce) can unsweetened coconut milk
3 tablespoons cornstarch
¾ cup sugar
¼ teaspoon kosher salt
2 eggs
1 teaspoon vanilla extract

1. Preheat oven to 350°. Spread coconut on a baking pan and toast in the oven 3 minutes. Stir coconut around so it will toast evenly, then bake 1 to 2 minutes more, until golden brown. Set aside ¼ cup to sprinkle on finished cake.
2. Bring milk and coconut milk just to a boil in a heavy saucepan (preferably stainless steel).
3. Whisk cornstarch, sugar, salt, eggs, and vanilla together in a mixing bowl. Pour in hot milk mixture, whisking constantly. Return mixture to the saucepan and cook over low heat 1 minute, whisking occasionally. The custard must boil briefly to thicken correctly and to cook out the "raw" cornstarch taste. Stir in the ½ cup of toasted coconut.
4. Place custard in a metal or hard plastic container. Lightly press plastic wrap onto the surface of the custard to prevent a skin from forming on top, and refrigerate at least 30 minutes, or until cool.

   Notes:
   - For nondairy diets, substitute coconut milk or water for the milk in the custard.
   - The custard can be made with or without the coconut and used for a number of other desserts. Try lightening the texture with **Sweetened whipped cream** (2 parts custard to 1 part whipped cream) and layering with mangoes, papayas, or pineapples for a tropical trifle, or use as a filling for crêpes and serve with a pineapple sauce.

Beaujolais Nouveau Fête

Beaujolais Nouveau wine, named for the Beaujolais region in France, is made from Gamay grapes. This light and fruity red wine is unusual in that the wine is consumed young (*nouveau*) and at a cool temperature. Beaujolais Nouveau goes well with assertively flavored fish such as salmon and, in the United States, often makes an appearance on the Thanksgiving table.

Grill-smoked salmon with salsapesto

Mushroom rice pilaf

Artichokes with garlic, lemon, and red chile flakes

Green salad with fresh herb–mustard vinaigrette

Ciabatta bread

Upside-down pear-almond cake

Grill-smoked salmon
with salsapesto

Westerbeke guests rave about this dish. It requires using an outdoor grill with a fairly tight-fitting lid, such as a Weber, and produces such a delicious result that you may start grilling everything this way.

Serves 8

Simple brine (recipe follows)
Salsapesto (recipe follows)
8 (½- to ¾-inch-thick) salmon steaks
Wood chips for your barbecue

1. Make **Simple brine.** Chill before using.
2. Make **Salsapesto.**
3. Immerse salmon steaks in cold brine for 25 minutes, then drain well. Soak a handful of wood chips in cold water for at least 10 minutes.
4. Burn 3 or 4 double handfuls of charcoal briquettes or wood beyond the usual stage for cooking—they should be almost cooling off. Remove the grill grate (the part you actually cook on), scrub it well with a metal brush, and lightly spray or brush with oil. Push coals to one side. Close all vents on the grill. Drain wood chips and sprinkle them onto the coals. Spray or brush salmon steaks lightly with oil on the side you're going to place onto the grate first (usually the rib side).
5. When chips begin to smoke, place salmon on grate and replace grate. Salmon should not be directly over coals. Cover and cook 5 to 7 minutes, depending on thickness of fish and heat of grill.
6. When fish is firm throughout, remove immediately and serve. If fish needs more cooking time, turn over, replace cover, and cook another 2 or 3 minutes. Serve with salsapesto on the side.

   Notes:
   + Fruitwoods and hardwoods are best for smoking. I prefer the strong flavor of hickory, but apple is often used for seafood. Wood chips are available at drugstores (in the camping or barbecue sections) and at hardware and grocery stores.
   + If using very thin salmon steaks, such as tail pieces, brine for only 15 minutes.
   + Fish sticking to the grill can be a problem. Oil both fish and grill—lightly!—and you should get nice grill marks on your fish. A hot, well-seasoned grill is important. Use a spatula with a straight, sharp edge to get under the fish. When working with a really hot grill, I wear gloves to protect my hands.
   + The most common mistake when grilling fish is overcooking. Salmon should be just barely cooked in the center; any more and it will be dry. If in doubt, undercook. To test doneness, pull apart a piece of fish slightly and peek inside, or use an instant-read meat thermometer inserted into the thickest part of a salmon steak; it should read between 135° and 145°.
   + For large parties, try this do-ahead method: Undercook the fish somewhat, then lay it out on an oiled baking pan and pass it through a hot oven to finish cooking.

Simple brine

Makes about 1 quart

1 quart water
¼ cup kosher salt
¼ cup lightly packed light brown sugar

1. Bring water, salt, and sugar to a boil.
2. Remove from heat, allow to cool, and chill.

   Note:
   + For more on brine and its uses, see **All-purpose brine** in Essential Recipes.

Salsapesto

One day I was grilling salmon and wanted to make something full-flavored to go with it, something like a salsa or a pesto but not exactly either of those things. This is the sauce I came up with. Don't let the long ingredient list fool you—this is an easy recipe. Just wash, chop, measure, and mix.

Makes about 3 cups

2 cups peeled, seeded, and diced tomatoes
3 tablespoons pitted and chopped olives (green, black, or mixed)
½ teaspoon minced fresh garlic
½ teaspoon anchovy paste
¼ cup chopped fresh basil
⅔ cup chopped fresh Italian parsley
½ teaspoon dry oregano
½ teaspoon dry tarragon
2 tablespoons olive oil
1 tablespoon balsamic vinegar
1 tablespoon red wine vinegar
2 tablespoons thinly sliced green onions
1½ teaspoons kosher salt
¼ teaspoon black pepper
2 teaspoons capers (optional)
¼ teaspoon red chile flakes (optional)

1. Combine all ingredients in a mixing bowl. Stir and add more salt if necessary.

   Notes:
   + If you're short on time, don't peel the tomatoes, just core and dice them.
   + **Roasted tomatoes** can be used for this recipe.
   + Rinsing olives removes excess salt and softens the flavor somewhat.
   + For a vegetarian version (to serve with grilled tofu cutlets or kabobs), omit anchovy paste.
   + Use leftover salsapesto with grilled fish, chicken, or pork. Serve with toasted or grilled baguette slices for an appetizer.

Mushroom rice pilaf

The earthiness of mushrooms and a touch of soy sauce give white rice plenty of oomph.

Serves 6 to 8

2¼ cups vegetable stock*
1½ cups jasmine or long-grain white rice
1¼ cups (about 5 ounces) minced crimini mushrooms
1 tablespoon soy sauce
1 teaspoon kosher salt
1 teaspoon canola or salad oil

1. Bring stock to a boil. Add rice, mushrooms, soy sauce, salt, and oil. Whisk to combine.
2. Return to a boil, stir once, reduce heat, and cover. Simmer 15 minutes.
3. Remove from heat and let sit, covered, 5 minutes. Fluff with a fork.

* As a quick substitute for vegetable stock, try vegetarian chicken broth mix, available in the bulk foods section of natural foods stores. Whisk in 1 tablespoon for each cup of hot water.

Notes:
  + If using a rice cooker, just place everything in the cooker, mix well, and follow the manufacturer's instructions. Always use cold water to start.
  + Crimini (or Italian field) mushrooms are very young portobellos. They look like dark brown button mushrooms but have a lot more flavor.

Artichokes
with garlic, lemon, and red chile flakes

Frustrated with time-consuming methods of cooking artichokes, I came up with an easy recipe that can be made a day ahead. Because this dish is served at room temperature, it is great for a picnic or potluck meal.

Serves 8

8 artichokes
1½ tablespoons minced fresh garlic
¾ teaspoon black pepper
½ teaspoon red chile flakes
1¼ teaspoons kosher salt
Zest of 1 lemon
½ cup lemon juice
1 tablespoon red wine vinegar
½ cup olive oil

1. Cut off all but 1 inch of artichoke stems. Cut off about an inch of the pointed top. Cut artichoke in half vertically, from top to stem.
2. Immediately place artichoke halves into a large pot of salted water and bring to a boil. Cover, reduce heat, and simmer 15 to 20 minutes. Check for doneness by pushing a paring knife into the thickest part of the heart; if the knife goes in easily, remove artichokes from water immediately. Do not overcook. Cool to room temperature.
3. Whisk together remaining ingredients.
4. Using a spoon, scoop out and discard the hairy center of each artichoke half. Place artichokes in a bowl and pour dressing over them. Toss to coat well and marinate for about 1 hour or up to 24 hours. Serve at room temperature.

Green salad
with fresh herb–mustard vinaigrette

This salad's mustardy dressing takes me back to cooking in France. The fresh herbs and lemon juice add zip.

Serves 6 to 8

Fresh herb–mustard vinaigrette (recipe follows)
Tamari-roasted pumpkinseeds (page 208)
¾ pound mesclun mix, mixed baby greens, or winter mix

Your choice of any or all of the following:
1 carrot, grated
¼ pound alfalfa sprouts
½ English cucumber, sliced into thin rounds

1. Make **Fresh herb–mustard vinaigrette** and **Tamari-roasted pumpkinseeds**.
2. Place the greens in a bowl, and toss with just enough dressing to coat lightly. Arrange the other ingredients on top and around the sides.

Fresh herb–mustard vinaigrette

Makes 1½ cups

¼ teaspoon granulated garlic
½ cup chopped fresh parsley
1 tablespoon chopped fresh oregano
¼ cup smooth Dijon-style mustard
3 tablespoons white wine vinegar
½ teaspoon kosher salt
¼ teaspoon black pepper
2 tablespoons water
1 tablespoon lemon juice
1 teaspoon sugar
1 cup good olive oil or canola oil

1. Place all ingredients except oil in a food processor fitted with blade. With processor running, drizzle in oil until it is completely incorporated and vinaigrette is smooth. If you don't have a food processor, mix all the ingredients except the oil in a bowl. Then, while whisking quickly, slowly drizzle in oil until the vinaigrette is smooth.

   Notes:
   + For a more robust dressing, substitute basil for the parsley.
   + A blender can be used for this recipe. The result will be a smoother, more brightly colored dressing.

Ciabatta bread

This is my version of a wonderful artisan bread I buy locally. It has large, irregular holes inside and a wonderful toasted-nut aroma. The wet dough is "turned" rather than kneaded, to work in more flour and stiffen the dough. In Italian, ciabatta means "slipper," but the image these rustic loaves bring to mind is definitely more Grandpa's than Cinderella's.

Makes 2 (1-pound) loaves

2½ cups warm (about 100°) tap water
1 tablespoon kosher salt
1½ teaspoons active dry yeast
5¾ cups bread flour, preferably unbleached organic, divided

1. With a wooden spoon, stir water and salt in a large mixing bowl. Add yeast and stir to dissolve. Add 4½ cups of the bread flour and beat 30 seconds with a wooden spoon. Dough will be very wet.
2. Cover bowl with plastic wrap (wrap should not touch the dough) and let rise 1 hour in a warm place.
3. Spread ¾ cup of the flour on a large cookie sheet or a 17-by-11-inch baking pan, so it lightly covers the whole pan. Place dough on floured pan.
4. The dough is very sticky at this point, so use a little of the flour on the pan to rub on your hands if necessary. Pull the dough into a rectangle about 1 inch thick, so it almost fills the pan. Fold the long edge of the dough down to the middle of the dough. Fold the remaining sides to the middle (they will overlap). The process of folding the dough is more important than the shape.
5. Turn dough seam-side down and let rest 5 minutes, then repeat. Try not to push down on the dough, just pull and fold. The dough will stiffen, and much of the flour from the pan will be absorbed during this step. Cover dough with well-oiled plastic wrap and let rise 45 minutes in a warm place.
6. Spread out ¼ cup of the flour (about the size of the pan) on worksurface. Turn dough out and cut into 2 equal pieces. Clean baking pan and spread 2 tablespoons of flour on it.
7. Stretch out first piece of dough into a rough rectangle, about 13 by 9 inches. Fold ⅓ of one long edge into the center, then cover with the opposite edge, like folding a sheet of letterhead. Place loaf, seam side down, on floured pan. "Neaten" loaf by tucking any bulges of dough under the long sides. Handle as little as possible; preserving bubbles inside dough is important here. Repeat with other piece of dough and remaining 2 tablespoons. Dust loaves with a little of the flour from the table. Cover loaves with well-oiled plastic wrap and let rise in a warm place 45 minutes. Loaves should be tender and spring back when pressed lightly with your finger.
8. While bread is rising, preheat oven to 450° and place a baking pan on the bottom (floor) of the oven.

continued——→

Ciabatta bread

continued from previous page

9. Measure ½ cup of hot tap water. Remove plastic wrap and place bread in the oven. Immediately pour the hot water into the baking pan beneath (careful—it will boil vigorously!). Quickly close oven door. Add another ½ cup hot water every 2 minutes, 4 times in all. This is the crucial "steam" step that softens the crust, allowing the dough to expand and creating a light, crusty bread.

10. Bake loaves 15 minutes more, turn the pans front to back, and bake 8 to 10 minutes more, or until loaves are dark brown. Cool loaves on a rack.

    Notes:
    + A plastic dough scraper or bench knife (see Tools and Equipment) comes in handy for this recipe.
    + High-protein bread flour is preferable, but all-purpose flour can be substituted.
    + Precise measurements are especially important for this recipe. Use a 1 cup measure and flatten off the top every time. Do the same with measuring spoons.
    + A packet of active dry yeast contains 2¼ teaspoons yeast.
    + Although this bread is best when served the same day, it freezes well: after baking and cooling, wrap loaves well in plastic wrap and freeze for up to a month. Thaw at room temperature for 1 hour and recrisp in preheated 400° oven 6 to 8 minutes, or slice and toast individual pieces.
    + Older ovens may not heat up to 450°, even if the dial is set to 450°. Use an oven thermometer to verify temperature. If temperature is low, increase baking time and check doneness according to the final step.

Upside-down pear-almond cake

This dessert is a combination of a very rich almond cake and caramelized pears. After baking and cooling, the cake is inverted and cut into wedges. Serve it with a dollop of whipped cream or a scoop of vanilla ice cream.

Makes 1 (9-inch round) single-layer cake

¾ cup plus 1 tablespoon sugar, divided
3½ cups peeled, diced firm pears (3 to 4 Bartlett or d'Anjou)
Pinch of salt
3 eggs
¾ cup (6 ounces) almond paste
¼ cup (½ stick) unsalted butter
2 teaspoons vanilla extract
3 tablespoons all-purpose flour

1. Preheat oven to 350°.
2. Cut a circle of parchment paper to fit inside the bottom of cake pan. Lightly oil the pan, lay the parchment paper circle inside the pan, and lightly oil the paper.
3. Place ½ cup of the sugar in a large saucepan over high heat. Watch for sugar to dissolve as pan gets hot. As sugar dissolves and darkens around the pan edges, stir with a wooden spoon. When sugar is completely dissolved, keep stirring until it turns brown. Caramel may smoke a bit at this point. Immediately add pears and salt, and continue stirring.
4. Reduce heat to medium and cook pears, stirring frequently. The pears will release their juice. Keep cooking and stirring until most of the juice has cooked away and pears are tender, about 8 to 10 minutes. Pour pears and caramel into prepared pan and spread pears evenly over the bottom.
5. Place eggs, uncracked and in their shells, in a bowl. Cover with hot tap water and let sit for about 10 minutes.
6. Place almond paste and butter in a bowl and microwave for 30 seconds on high power until butter is melted and almond paste is hot and soft. Place almond paste-butter mixture in food processor fitted with the blade; process 10 seconds, or until smooth. Transfer mixture to a bowl, add vanilla and flour, and stir just until combined. Pour batter over pears to cover completely. Tap the pan lightly on work surface so the batter will settle around the pears.
7. Bake 25 minutes, or until top is lightly browned. Cool ½ hour. Run a paring knife around the pan to loosen the cake, then turn it out onto a plate. Peel off parchment paper and cut into wedges.

   Note:
   + This cake can also be made with apples. To make the cake with soft fruits such as figs, peaches, or nectarines, sprinkle the prepared cake pan with sugar and omit the caramel.

Virgin of Guadalupe Fiesta

DECEMBER 12

The legend of Our Lady of Guadalupe dates back to 1531. The story involves a man named Juan Diego and his vision of the Virgin Mary. Every year, Wendy Westerbeke brings out her wonderful collection of paintings, fabrics, and altars to honor the Virgin of Guadalupe with a celebration dinner. I created this menu for one of those parties.

Chicken mole poblano

Green rice

Succotash with hominy
and black beans

Spinach salad with jicama,
red onion, grapefruit, and
pumpkinseed dressing

Classic vanilla flan

Anise seed biscochitos

Chicken mole poblano

Mole is one of the crowning achievements of Latin American cuisine. This version is called *poblano* because it is in the style of Puebla, Mexico. The combination of cooking methods and ingredients gives this dish an incredible depth of flavor I find both familiar and mysterious.

Serves 6 to 8

2 (3-pound) chickens, each cut into 8 pieces
3 cups **Roasted-chicken stock** (recipe follows) or canned low-salt chicken broth
1 quart **Mole poblano sauce** (recipe follows)
1 tablespoon plus 1 teaspoon kosher salt
2 teaspoons black pepper
¼ cup canola or salad oil
12 to 15 flour tortillas
2 tablespoons sesame seeds, lightly toasted

1. Use chicken backs and necks to make **Roasted-chicken stock**. Make **Mole poblano sauce**.
2. Season remaining chicken pieces with the salt and pepper, then set aside for about 20 minutes. In a large pan, heat the oil over high heat until it is almost smoking. Sear the chicken pieces until browned all over. Pour off the oil.
3. Add stock and mole sauce to pan and mix well. Bring to a boil, reduce heat, and simmer, covered, 30 to 45 minutes. Chicken should be tender but not falling apart. If the sauce seems thin, remove the chicken and simmer the sauce, uncovered, 5 to 10 minutes more to reduce it a bit. Warm tortillas in oven or microwave, or on griddle, while mixture simmers.
4. Sprinkle each serving with sesame seeds. Serve tortillas on the side.

Roasted-chicken stock

Makes 1½ quarts

Chicken backs and necks from 2 chickens above
About 2 quarts water

1. Preheat oven to 350°.
2. Lightly oil a baking pan. Place chicken backs and necks on pan in one layer and roast 20 to 30 minutes, or until well browned.
3. Place roasted chicken parts in a stockpot, add the water, and bring to a boil. Skim off any fat and scum that come to the surface and discard.
4. Reduce heat and simmer 1 hour, uncovered. Strain before using.

   Notes:
   + When asking the butcher to cut up whole chickens, be sure to ask for the back and necks, and use for chicken stock.
   + Using a stock made from roasted chicken parts gives the finished mole a slightly deeper flavor. If you have time, make an even more richly flavored stock by roasting 1 carrot, 1 small onion (both peeled and chopped), 2 stalks chopped celery, and 3 cloves garlic with the chicken parts. Then add everything to the stockpot.

Mole poblano sauce

This may well be the most challenging recipe in this book, but if the complex flavor of real mole interests you, try it! You'll find this sauce far superior to anything you can buy, and there will plenty left over to freeze for other meals.

Makes about 1 gallon

2 quarts **Three chile purée** (page 210)
¼ cup canola oil
1 large yellow or white onion, chopped
¼ cup garlic cloves
½ cup sesame seeds, toasted
1 tablespoon coriander seeds
2 teaspoons black pepper
¼ teaspoon ground cloves
1½ teaspoons anise or fennel seeds
½ cup dry-roasted peanuts
½ cup whole or sliced almonds, toasted
1 cup raisins
1 cup crumbled yellow corn tortilla chips
2 cups canned diced tomatoes in their juice
2 (3.1-ounce) rounds Mexican-style chocolate*
1½ cups strong coffee
1½ tablespoons kosher salt
3 cups chicken stock, vegetable stock, or water

1. Make **Three chile purée.**
2. In a large stockpot, heat oil until it SHIMMERS. Add onion and garlic and cook, stirring often, until lightly browned.
3. Add sesame seeds, coriander seeds, pepper, cloves, and anise or fennel seeds. Stir 5 to 10 seconds, until you can really smell the spices. Add chile purée, peanuts, almonds, raisins, tortilla chips, and tomatoes to stockpot. Bring mixture to a boil, reduce heat, and simmer, covered, 30 minutes. The mixture will be fairly thick, so stir often to prevent it from sticking to the bottom of the pan.
4. Remove stockpot from heat. Add chocolate, coffee, and salt, stirring well to melt chocolate.
5. In a blender, purée the mixture in 4 or 5 batches until completely smooth, using some of the stock in each batch.

Mexican-style chocolate is available in many grocery stores and Latin markets. Look for Ibarra or Majordomo brands.

continued——>

Chicken mole poblano

continued from previous page

Notes:

+ If you don't have fresh coffee on hand, stir 1 tablespoon plus 2 teaspoons powdered coffee (I use Folgers decaf crystals) into 1½ cups hot water.

+ Either buy toasted nuts or toast them yourself in a preheated 350° oven for 4 to 6 minutes, or until light brown.

+ If you like spicy food, add half of a 7-ounce can of chipotle chiles in adobo sauce to the stockpot with the chile purée and other ingredients. This will produce a very spicy sauce that will mellow a bit when cooked with chicken.

+ This recipe is time consuming, so if you have big enough pots and pans, make a double batch and freeze the extra. You'll be glad you did!

+ To make vegetarian mole sauce, simply use vegetable stock or water in place of chicken stock. Use vegetarian mole sauce with crispy tofu cubes (see **Hot-sweet tofu** for method) or roasted vegetables.

Green rice

I like to change the color and the flavor of rice dishes, depending on the other dishes I am serving. Green rice offers a nice contrast to dark-brown mole sauce.

Serves 6 to 8

1 small bunch spinach
2¼ cups water or vegetable stock*
2 teaspoons kosher salt
½ jalapeño pepper with seeds
3 cloves garlic
2 tablespoons canola oil
1½ cups jasmine or long-grain white rice

1. Blend spinach, water, salt, jalapeño, and garlic in a blender for 3 to 5 seconds; the spinach should still have a little texture.
2. In medium saucepan over medium-high heat, heat oil until it SHIMMERS. Add rice and cook, stirring, 5 to 8 minutes, until grains are lightly browned.
3. Add the spinach-water mixture and bring to a boil, stirring occasionally. Reduce heat to low, cover, and simmer 15 minutes.
4. Remove pan from heat and let sit, covered, 5 minutes. Fluff with a fork before serving.

* As a quick substitute for vegetable stock, try vegetarian chicken broth mix, available in the bulk foods section of natural foods stores. Whisk in 1 tablespoon for each cup of hot water.

Notes:
+ If using a rice cooker, do not sauté the rice and use only 1 tablespoon oil.
+ Many greens can be substituted for the spinach, or added to it for more vitamins and green color. Try parsley, arugula, mustard greens, or chard.

Succotash with hominy
and black beans

Originally a Southern dish, succotash has many variations. This simple, hearty side dish has contrasting colors and earthy flavors that, like a stew, just get better with reheating.

Serves 6

1½ cups **Black beans** (recipe follows), or 1 (15-ounce) can, rinsed and drained
2 tablespoons olive oil
½ yellow onion, diced
2 red bell peppers, diced
1 tablespoon minced fresh garlic
1 (15-ounce) can white or yellow hominy, rinsed and drained
1 (8-ounce) can diced tomatoes in their juice
1 teaspoon kosher salt
¼ teaspoon black pepper
⅛ teaspoon cayenne pepper
¼ teaspoon ground celery seed

1. Make **Black beans.**
2. Heat the oil over high heat in a large sauté pan, until it is almost smoking. Add onion and peppers, and stir rapidly for a minute, or until slightly browned.
3. Stir in garlic, then remaining ingredients. Cook 3 to 5 minutes, stirring often, until heated through.

   Notes:
   + Substitute frozen baby lima beans, butter beans, or cooked green beans for the black beans. Cooking time will be slightly longer.
   + Try adding ¼ cup whipping cream or ¼ cup **Three chile purée** and heat through at the end.

Black beans
½ cup dried black beans
2 cups water

1. Check beans and remove any stones; rinse well.
2. Bring water and beans to a boil in a small saucepan. Reduce heat to very low and simmer, covered, 45 minutes to 1 hour or until tender.
3. Drain well in a colander.

   Note:
   + Cooked black beans freeze well.

Spinach salad with jicama,
red onion, grapefruit, and pumpkinseed dressing

I often make this salad with romaine lettuce instead of spinach. Either way, it always disappears quickly.

Serves 6 to 8

Pumpkinseed dressing (recipe follows)
¾ pound fresh spinach, preferably baby organic
½ small (softball-size) jicama, peeled and cut into "matchsticks"
2 ruby grapefruits, peeled, seeded, and cut into sections
⅓ cup very thinly sliced red onion
Tamari-roasted pumpkinseeds for garnish (optional)

1. **Make Pumpkinseed dressing.**
2. Toss spinach with enough dressing to coat leaves well.
3. Place dressed greens in a serving bowl. Arrange jicama and grapefruit sections around the sides, top with red onion, and sprinkle with more roasted pumpkinseeds, if desired.

Pumpkinseed dressing

Makes 2½ cups

½ cup **Tamari-roasted pumpkinseeds**
3 tablespoons seasoned rice wine vinegar
½ cup water
⅓ cup lime juice
1 small bunch green onions
½ bunch roughly chopped cilantro
1 tablespoon minced fresh garlic
2 teaspoons kosher salt
1 small jalapeño, with seeds, roughly chopped
1 tablespoon sugar
½ cups canola oil

1. Make **Tamari-roasted pumpkinseeds.**
2. Place pumpkinseeds, vinegar, water, and lime juice in a blender and blend on high speed until smooth, about 15 seconds.
3. Add green onions, cilantro, garlic, salt, jalapeño, and sugar. Blend again until smooth, about 5 seconds.
4. With the motor running, add oil in a thin stream until it is fully incorporated. (See EMULSIFY in Resources: Glossary.)

   Note:
   + Do not run the blender too long or the dressing will warm up and the flavors will diminish.

Classic vanilla flan

This is my version of the famous Mexican dessert. The "trembly" appearance, the soft texture, the vanilla flavor—sometimes you can't improve on tradition. Flan must be made the day before it is served, so the moisture of the custard will dissolve the caramel into a sauce.

Serves 8

Caramel (recipe follows)
3 cups whole milk, divided
¾ cup sugar
¼ teaspoon table salt
6 large eggs
1 egg yolk
2 teaspoons vanilla extract
32 fresh tangerine segments, for garnish

1. Make **Caramel** and prepare ramekins as directed.
2. Preheat oven to 350°.
3. Bring 2 cups of the milk, sugar, and salt to a boil in a small saucepan. Remove from heat.
4. Whisk together remaining 1 cup milk, eggs, and egg yolk, then whisk into hot liquid. Remove from heat and stir in vanilla. Pour custard through a mesh strainer into prepared ramekins, leaving about ½ inch of space at the top of each one.
5. Place the ramekins at least ¾ inch apart in a high-sided baking pan. Carefully add hot tap water to the pan (don't splash any water into the ramekins!) to a depth of ½ inch. Cover pan with aluminum foil and bake 20 minutes.
6. Carefully—to avoid hot steam—lift foil and jiggle a ramekin. The flan should move as one mass. If too "liquidy," bake another 5 to 7 minutes. Flan must be cooked enough to set but never so much that you see bubbles in it. Be patient.
7. When flans are done, remove from pan and let cool to room temperature. Refrigerate overnight. To serve, run a paring knife around the inside of ramekins and turn flans out onto small plates, letting all the caramel run out on top of each serving.
8. Arranged tangerine segments around each flan.

    Note:
    + Depending on the season, flan can be garnished with fresh berries, mangoes, papayas, apricots, kiwis, or star fruit.

Caramel

This recipe involves what is called the "dry method" of making caramel. I find it much less fussy than the classic method of adding water to the sugar, then cooking it off while brushing the pan with water.

Makes enough for 8 ramekins

1¾ cups sugar

1. Set out 8 (6-ounce) ramekins or custard cups.
2. Heat a heavy saucepan on high heat until very hot.
3. Add sugar. Watch carefully. When sugar begins to melt and brown around the pan's edges (which can happen immediately if your pan is very hot), stir with a wooden spoon until all sugar has melted and is medium brown.
4. Remove pan from heat. Pour just enough caramel into each ramekin to barely cover the bottom. Work quickly, or the caramel will harden.

   Notes:
   + Be extremely careful with caramel—it is very hot!
   + To clean the pan, fill with hot tap water and let sit for 10 minutes. Repeat until caramel dissolves.

Anise seed biscochitos

Biscochitos are similar to Mexican wedding cookies, with anise seeds instead of nuts. They have the flavor of licorice, a pleasantly sandy texture, and a coating of cinnamon sugar. Biscochitos can be served alone, with coffee, or alongside vanilla flan.

Makes 36 cookies

1 cup melted unsalted butter
1¾ cup sugar, divided
1 egg
¼ cup cream sherry
3 cups all-purpose flour
1½ teaspoons baking powder
½ teaspoon kosher salt
1 tablespoon anise seeds
1 teaspoon cinnamon

1. Preheat oven to 325°.
2. Mix butter and ¾ cup of the sugar in a mixing bowl with an electric mixer. Add egg and sherry, mixing well.
3. Sift flour with baking powder and salt, then add all at once with anise seeds to the butter mixture, mixing on low speed just until combined.
4. Stir together cinnamon and remaining 1 cup sugar. Spread on a large sheet of waxed paper. Using a tablespoon, roll dough by hand into balls about the size of small walnuts. Roll balls in cinnamon-sugar mixture and place on a baking pan lined with parchment paper.
5. Bake 12 to 15 minutes, or until light brown.

Notes:
+ Cookies can also be rolled in powdered sugar just after baking, instead of in cinnamon-sugar mixture before baking.
+ To make a cookie with more anise flavor throughout (especially if you don't like eating whole seeds), grind anise seeds briefly in an electric spice or coffee mill.

Winter Menus

New Year's Eve
Hors d'oeuvre Buffet

Chinese New Year Party

Valentine's Day Dinner

Carnaval Celebration

New Year's Eve Hors d'oeuvre Buffet

New Year's Eve is a holiday associated with indulgence. Why buck tradition? Serve this menu of appetizers for an elegant buffet, or pick one recipe to whet the appetite for another menu. Good Champagne pairs nicely with these dishes, besides being customary on this night of nights.

Wild-mushroom crostini with white truffle oil

Blackened shrimp

Oysters with fennel cream, bread crumbs, and Parmesan cheese

Artichoke-corn fritters with herb mayonnaise

Focaccia canapés with garlic cream and red pepper–olive spread

Chocolate lava cakes with vanilla ice cream

Wild-mushroom crostini
with white truffle oil

The smell of wild mushrooms cooking with fresh garlic is reason enough to try this recipe. Add the crunch of toasted baguette slices and the earthy aroma of truffle oil, and you have an unforgettable appetizer.

Serves 10/Makes 20

½ pound mixed wild mushrooms (such as chanterelle, porcini, oyster, crimini, or shiitake)
2 tablespoons unsalted butter
1 teaspoon minced fresh garlic
¼ cup dry white wine
¾ teaspoon kosher salt
¼ teaspoon black pepper
1 thin baguette
Good olive oil
2 tablespoons white truffle oil

1. Thinly slice mushrooms. In a medium sauté pan over medium heat, heat butter until it bubbles. Add mushrooms and garlic, and stir until mushrooms wilt but are not browned, about 2 minutes. Add wine; cook and stir another 2 minutes, or until most of liquid has cooked away. Remove from heat and season with salt and pepper.
2. Preheat oven to 300°.
3. Slice baguette into ¼-inch rounds, brush lightly with olive oil, and toast on a baking pan about 10 minutes, or until crisp and very lightly browned.
4. Place a tablespoon of mushroom mixture on top of each slice. Transfer crostini to a serving plate, drizzle with a little truffle oil, and serve immediately. Crostini can also be kept warm in the oven 5 minutes before adding truffle oil and serving.

   Notes:
   + A little truffle oil goes a long way, plus it's expensive. Buy the smallest bottle you can find. If possible, select an oil with truffle "essence" instead of "aroma" or "flavoring." Truffle oil has an assertive aroma and flavor. Drizzle it on warm foods such as pastas, pizza, grilled or braised meat, mashed potatoes, potato soup, or scrambled eggs.
   + If you're a truffle lover, use 3 tablespoons truffle oil.
   + Fresh herbs are a delicious addition to the mushroom mixture. Try ½ teaspoon chopped oregano, 2 teaspoons chopped parsley, or both.
   + Both the crostini and the mushroom mixture can be made ahead.

Blackened shrimp

Blackened fish originated in New Orleans and gained popularity nationwide. "Blackening" packs a lot of flavor and works equally well with chicken, red snapper, halibut, or cod.

Serves 10

Blackening spice mix (recipe follows)
1½ pounds shrimp (size 16 to 20), peeled and deveined
¼ pound (1 stick) unsalted butter, melted
12 lemon wedges (from 2 lemons) for garnish

1. Make **Blackening spice mix.**
2. Toss shrimp in melted butter, then coat with the spice mixture.
3. Heat a heavy sauté pan, preferably cast iron, over high heat until very hot. Add shrimp in batches, no more than will fit in one layer. Cook about 1 minute, then turn and cook about 30 seconds. Check for doneness by cutting a shrimp in half at the thickest point. It should be just barely cooked through. Garnish with lemon wedges and serve immediately.

Blackening spice mix

Makes about ⅓ cup

1 tablespoon dried thyme
1½ teaspoons dried oregano
3 bay leaves
1 tablespoon celery salt
1 tablespoon granulated garlic
1 tablespoon granulated onion
3 tablespoons paprika
1½ teaspoons white pepper
½ teaspoon sugar
⅛ teaspoon cayenne pepper

1. Grind the thyme, oregano, and bay leaves to a fine powder in an electric spice or coffee mill.
2. Combine all ingredients and mix well.

Oysters with fennel cream,
bread crumbs, and Parmesan cheese

Along with champagne and caviar, oysters are synonymous with luxury. This fennel cream is rich, but delicate enough that it doesn't mask the mollusks' briny flavor.

Serves 10/Makes 20

Fennel cream (recipe follows)
¼ cup finely grated fresh Parmesan or Asiago cheese
¼ cup plus 2 tablespoons dry white bread crumbs
20 oysters, medium to large size

1. Make **Fennel cream.**
2. Make crust mixture by stirring together cheese and bread crumbs.
3. Preheat oven to 400°. Scrub oysters under running water and place on a baking pan. Bake 6 minutes, or until a few oysters are open. Remove all oysters from oven. Shuck oysters (see Notes).
4. Place oysters on the half shell on a baking pan. Top each one with about a tablespoonful of the fennel cream, or enough to cover oyster completely. Top fennel cream with a big pinch of crust mixture. Bake 6 to 8 minutes, or until crust is lightly browned.

Notes:
+ I prefer panko, or Japanese-style bread crumbs.
+ Look for Hog Island, Fanny Bay, bluepoint, or Belon oysters.
+ When shucking oysters, always use an oyster knife, wrap a towel around your left hand (or the hand holding the oyster), or wear a sturdy glove on that hand. Hold the oyster firmly on a stable surface while twisting the oyster knife into the "hinge" where the two shells come together. Once the knife is inside, sweep it around to free the oyster from its shell, then remove top shell. Sweep knife below the oyster to free it from bottom shell, or "cup," leaving oyster sitting in the cup. Remove any shell pieces.
+ Rock salt can be used in this recipe either for baking or for presentation. For baking, fill the pan to a depth of ½ inch with rock salt and nestle oyster shells in salt. For presentation, spread a thin layer of rock salt in your serving dish and nestle oysters in the salt.
+ If you want to splurge, top each oyster with a little caviar just before serving. Sturgeon, or "true," caviar ranges in quality and cost. From least to most expensive types, they are sevruga, osetra, and beluga.

Fennel cream

Makes 1¼ cups

½ large fennel bulb, roughly chopped (about 1 cup)
¾ cup whipping cream
¼ cup water
2 cloves garlic
½ teaspoon kosher salt
¼ teaspoon black pepper
2 teaspoons lemon juice
1 tablespoon chopped fennel leaves

1. Trim off root end of fennel bulb. Wash bulb and leaves. Remove leaves from stalks. Discard stalks. Chop leaves and set aside.
2. Place fennel bulb, cream, water, garlic, and salt in a small saucepan and bring to a boil. Reduce heat to very low, cover, and cook 20 minutes. Watch the cream carefully—it loves to boil over!
3. Place cream mixture in a blender with pepper and lemon juice. Cover blender with cloth to prevent hot mixture from spraying. Blend on low speed and gradually increase to high speed for 10 seconds, or until completely smooth. Stir in fennel leaves.

   Note:
   + If you enjoy the "licoricey" flavor of fennel, stir in a tablespoon of Pernod or Ricard (anise-flavored liqueurs) with the fennel leaves.

Artichoke-corn fritters
with herb mayonnaise

They're hot, crisp, and bursting with flavor. They're dipped in a tart, refreshing sauce. You bite in, then follow with cold Champagne. Can we have New Year's Eve all year long?

Serves 10/Makes 20

Herb mayonnaise (recipe follows)
1 cup frozen corn, thawed and well drained
1 egg
1 cup buttermilk
1 cup all-purpose flour
½ cup cornmeal
1 tablespoon kosher salt
½ teaspoon white pepper
1 cup good amber beer
Canola or peanut oil for deep-frying
1½ (8-ounce) packages frozen artichoke hearts, thawed
½ cup flour

1. Make **Herb mayonnaise.**
2. Place corn in blender with egg and buttermilk. Blend 8 seconds or until smooth.
3. Sift the flour, then place in a bowl with cornmeal, salt, and pepper. Whisk in corn-buttermilk mixture, then beer.
4. Pour oil to a depth of 2 inches in a heavy, deep pot. Heat oil to 350° on a deep-frying thermometer. (Or check temperature by making a small test fritter from batter. It should bubble vigorously and float after about 10 seconds.)
5. Coat artichokes with dusting flour, no more than 8 at a time. Shake off excess flour, then dip, one by one, into batter. Carefully drop individually into hot oil. Fry fritters until they float and turn light brown. Drain on paper towels. Serve immediately with herb mayonnaise.

   Notes:
   + Artichoke hearts are also available canned in water. A 14-ounce can contains about the same number of artichoke hearts as an 8-ounce frozen package. Drain well before using.
   + If artichoke hearts have any tough outer leaves, remove and discard them.

Herb mayonnaise

This cold sauce is lightened by replacing half of the mayonnaise with sour cream. It is delicious with cold poached salmon or cold chicken breasts, or as a dipping sauce for fried vegetables such as the artichokes I've paired it with here.

Makes 1¾ cups

½ teaspoon celery seed
¼ cup minced red onion
½ cup finely chopped Italian parsley leaves
1 tablespoon minced fresh tarragon
½ cup minced green onions
1 tablespoon minced capers
1 tablespoon caper juice
¾ cup mayonnaise
¾ cup sour cream
¼ cup lemon juice
Pinch of cayenne pepper
1 teaspoon kosher salt
½ teaspoon dry mustard

1. Grind celery seed in an electric spice or coffee mill.
2. Whisk together all ingredients.

Notes:
+ This sauce can be lightened even more by replacing the sour cream with nonfat yogurt.
+ Celery salt (which does not need to be ground) may be substituted for celery seed. Decrease kosher salt to ¾ teaspoon if using celery salt.

Focaccia canapés
with garlic cream and red pepper–olive spread

This is a wonderful appetizer with layers of flavor and components you can use in many ways. To start, you'll need a sheet of focaccia bread. Use my recipe, or buy a good-quality sheet.

Makes 48 triangles

Braised garlic cream (page 186)
Red pepper-olive spread (recipe follows)
1 sheet **Focaccia bread** (page 93)

1. Make **Braised garlic cream** and **Red pepper-olive spread**.
2. Cut an 8-by-5-inch rectangle from the focaccia sheet, then cut each rectangle in half horizontally.
3. Place the two focaccia rectangles cut-side up and spread each rectangle lightly with ½ cup of the **Braised garlic cream.**
4. Cut each rectangle into 12 pieces, then cut each piece in half on the diagonal.
5. Top each triangle with 1 teaspoon **Red pepper-olive spread** and a **Braised garlic clove** (page 194).

   Notes:
   + This sauce can be used on pizza, in lasagna, over stuffed pasta shells (on top of marinara sauce), or under a grilled chicken breast topped with roasted pepper strips (see **Roasted red peppers** in Essential Recipes) dressed with olive oil and a splash of balsamic. Make a garlicky Alfredo sauce using this recipe and adding some Asiago cheese and a dash of black pepper; toss with spaghettini, linguini, or fettuccini.
   + Although it is not essential, I usually strain the sauce to remove any remaining hard ends of the cloves.
   + I usually make this recipe with the quick whipping cream version of the braised garlic cream on page 186. Make this recipe vegan by using **Cashew cream sauce** instead.

Red pepper–olive spread

Makes 1½ cups

1 large red bell pepper
1 poblano chile or green bell pepper
½ cup pitted Kalamata or Niçoise olives, rinsed, drained, and minced
3 tablespoons olive oil
1½ teaspoons minced fresh garlic
1 tablespoon balsamic vinegar
2 teaspoons red wine vinegar
1 teaspoon fresh or dried oregano
1 tablespoon finely chopped fresh basil
½ teaspoon kosher salt
½ teaspoon black pepper
¼ teaspoon red chile flakes or ⅛ teaspoon cayenne pepper

1. Roast, peel, seed, and mince the peppers (for roasting method, see **Roasted red peppers** in Essential Recipes).
2. Combine all ingredients in a small bowl.

   Note:
   + The flavor of this spread is reminiscent of the one used in an Italian muffuletta sandwich. Try it on sandwiches, grilled vegetables, chicken breasts, crackers spread with a little cream cheese, or sautéed tofu cutlets.

Chocolate lava cakes
with vanilla ice cream

These chocolate cakes with a molten center are one of our most popular desserts. In fact, I considered renaming them when a returning guest called and requested the chocolate "love" cakes. I was lucky to have Master Pastry Chef Bo Friberg as an instructor in cooking school, and his recipe, from *The Professional Pastry Chef*, 3rd edition, inspired this one. The method is simple, the result sublime.

Serves 6

5 ounces bittersweet chocolate
2 ounces unsweetened chocolate
5 ounces (1¼ sticks) unsalted butter
3 tablespoons cornstarch
¾ cup plus 2 tablespoons sugar
4 eggs
4 egg yolks
1 tablespoon rum or brandy
Oil or butter for coating ramekins
Flour for dusting ramekins
1½ pints vanilla ice cream

1. Pour about ¾ inch water in the bottom of a double boiler, making certain top pan will not touch water. Bring the water to a boil, then reduce heat to simmer. Chop bittersweet and unsweetened chocolate into small pieces and place in the top of double boiler with butter and place over boiling water. Stir occasionally with a rubber spatula until chocolate and butter are completely melted and smooth. Remove from heat.
2. Sift cornstarch and sugar into a large bowl. In a medium bowl, whisk together the eggs, egg yolks, and rum or brandy, then whisk egg mixture into the cornstarch-sugar mixture all at once. Whisk in the chocolate-butter mixture.
3. Cover and chill batter at least 2 hours, or overnight, before using.
4. Preheat oven to 350°. Lightly oil or butter and flour six (6-ounce) ramekins or small soufflé dishes. Place ½ cup batter in each ramekin (a 4-ounce ice cream scooper dipped in hot water works nicely for this). Bake until barely risen and cracked on top, 10 to 14 minutes.
5. Cool about 8 minutes before serving. Unmold onto plates and serve a scoop of ice cream on the side, or serve right in ramekins, with a scoop of ice cream on top.

   Notes:
   + Bake the cakes just until they have risen and cracked, leaving the core gooey. If in doubt whether cakes are done, underbake them. If they're cooked all the way through, they're not lava cakes!
   + Ceramic ramekins with smooth insides work best.
   + Just about any flavor of ice cream is good with these cakes.
   + Lava cakes reheat beautifully in a microwave.

Chinese New Year Party

Originally an agricultural holiday marking the end of one growing season and the beginning of another, Chinese New Year is celebrated in much of Asia. Although it started as a fifteen-day celebration, today it is often scaled down to three days. Many rituals are observed during this period, such as a thorough housecleaning, the settling of all debts, the offering of sweets to the god of the kitchen, and a large family dinner. This menu includes some of the most popular Asian-inspired dishes from the Ranch.

Pen Leng's chow mein

Eggplant with hoisin and
browned-garlic dressing

Hot-sweet tofu

Tilapia with pan-Asian
ginger sauce

Cambodian coleslaw

Gingered ice cream
with sesame crisps

Pen Leng's chow mein

Pen Leng has worked in the Ranch kitchen for more than twenty years. Originally from Cambodia, she has inspired some of the best Asian dishes on our menus. This chow mein is a good example: authentic, simple, and satisfying. As with all high-heat cooking, it is important to have your ingredients ready before starting this recipe.

Serves 10 to 12

1 pound rice noodles (pad thai noodles)*
2 tablespoons soy sauce
2 teaspoons minced fresh garlic
¼ cup plus 3 tablespoons canola or salad oil, divided
3 eggs
½ teaspoon white pepper
1 teaspoon kosher salt
½ small yellow onion, thinly sliced
1 small carrot, peeled and grated
¼ pound mung bean sprouts
4 green onions, thinly sliced, for garnish

1. Bring a gallon of water to a boil. Add noodles to boiling water, cook for 2 to 3 minutes (see package directions, as cooking time varies according to type and thickness of noodles). Do not overcook. Drain.
2. Combine soy sauce, garlic, and ¼ cup of the oil in a large bowl. Add hot noodles and toss well; spread out on a large baking pan to cool.
3. Beat eggs with pepper and salt, and set aside.
4. Heat the 3 tablespoons oil until almost smoking in a large sauté pan or wok. Add onions and stir quickly for about 20 seconds. Add carrot and sprouts, then egg mixture. Stir quickly to combine, then add noodles. Stir 3 or 4 minutes more, or until noodles are well coated with egg and heated through. Sprinkle with green onions and serve immediately, or cover, keep warm, and serve up to 20 minutes later.

* Rice or pad thai noodles are available in Asian markets or the Asian foods section of some grocery stores. There are three common sizes: thin, medium, and wide. Thin or medium noodles are best for this recipe.

Notes:
+ Egg noodles made specifically for chow mein, spaghetti or spaghettini noodles, and rice or mung bean noodles all work well for this recipe.
+ Many Asian recipes use peanut oil for frying and wok cooking because it can withstand high heat without burning. Canola oil also resists burning and has a more neutral flavor.
+ This recipe yields more servings than the others in this menu because it is based on one (1-pound) bag of noodles, which are quite challenging to break apart when dry. You may have leftovers, but not for long.
+ Either drain noodles and use immediately, or drain, rinse with cold water, drain again, and use as needed. The latter is especially handy if noodles get slightly overcooked, or when cooking for large numbers of people, when it is important to get as much done ahead as possible.

Roasted eggplant
with hoisin and browned-garlic dressing

The toasty flavor of browned garlic and the sweetness of hoisin sauce are combined with meltingly tender roasted eggplant in this celebration of Asian flavors.

Serves 8

2 medium eggplants
1½ teaspoons kosher salt
Hoisin and browned-garlic dressing (recipe follows)
2 tablespoons canola oil
1 teaspoon black pepper
Chopped chives or green onion for garnish

1. Wash and dry eggplants. Trim stem ends and cut each eggplant in half (through the middle, not end to end). Cut each half lengthwise into 6 wedges. In a large bowl, toss wedges with salt to coat. Let sit 10 minutes.
2. Preheat oven to 350°. Make **Hoisin and browned-garlic dressing**.
3. Toss eggplants with oil and pepper to coat and place on lightly oiled (or parchment paper–lined) baking pans. Roast eggplants 14 to 16 minutes, or until soft but not mushy.
4. Allow eggplants to cool slightly, then place in a large bowl. Add dressing and, using a rubber spatula, gently turn eggplants to coat.
5. Arrange eggplants on a platter and sprinkle with chives or green onion.

Hoisin and browned-garlic dressing

1 tablespoon canola oil
3 tablespoons minced fresh garlic
1½ tablespoons dry white wine, sake, or water
3 tablespoons hoisin sauce
3 tablespoons rice wine vinegar
1½ teaspoons soy sauce

1. Heat oil in a small saucepan over high heat until very hot but not smoking. Add garlic and stir, scraping pan constantly with a metal spatula, until garlic is well browned. Browning the garlic goes quickly and there is a fine line between well browned and burned, so have the wine measured and ready.
2. Remove pan from heat and add wine—carefully!—to stop cooking. Scrape browned garlic into a bowl and add the hoisin sauce, rice wine vinegar, and soy sauce. Mix well and set aside.

Hot-sweet tofu

High-protein, low-calorie tofu can replace meat in many recipes. This sweet and spicy dish goes together quickly, and the tofu has a wonderful crunchy coating.

Serves 6 to 8

2 (14-ounce) packages extra-firm tofu
1½ teaspoons kosher salt
¾ cup canola oil
¾ cup cornstarch
½ cup sweet chili sauce*
3 green onions, thinly sliced

1. Drain the tofu and set each block on end, then cut into 3 slices. Sprinkle half of the salt over the slices, then turn them over, salt side down, and place on paper towels. Sprinkle with the remaining salt. Put more paper towels on top and press lightly to absorb water. Discard paper towels. Continue to blot tofu with more paper towels until it is almost dry. Cut tofu into ½-inch cubes.
2. Heat oil in a large sauté pan over medium-high heat until it Shimmers. Toss cubes with cornstarch and fry immediately; do not coat more cubes than you can fry at one time. Fry cubes in hot oil until light brown all over, turning once or twice. Remove tofu to paper towels to blot excess oil. Repeat for the rest of the cubes.
3. If serving immediately, put cubes in a bowl and toss with chili sauce and green onions. If serving later, remove cubes from paper towels to prevent sticking and reheat in a hot oven briefly before tossing with sauce.

* Sweet chili sauce is available in Asian markets or the Asian foods section of some grocery stores. Look for Mae Ploy brand.

Tilapia with pan-Asian ginger sauce

Here is a good example of how one recipe can be used as a building block for others. The method may look involved, but it's very simple: make the sweet-sour syrup, then the pan-Asian sauce, then cook the fish with the sauce.

Serves 8

1¼ cups **Pan-Asian ginger sauce** (recipe follows)
8 tilapia fillets
3 green onions, thinly sliced

1. Make **Pan-Asian ginger sauce.**
2. Lay tilapia fillets on an oiled baking pan and cover with the sauce. Marinate 15 to 20 minutes in the refrigerator. Preheat oven to 350°.
3. Bake fillets 8 to 10 minutes, or until fish flakes easily with a fork. To serve, arrange fillets on a platter, cover with sauce from the baking pan, and sprinkle with green onions.

   Note:
   + Tilapia is sustainably farmed, inexpensive, and usually sold as skinned and boned fillets.

Pan-Asian ginger sauce

By doubling this recipe, you'll have a sauce that can be the basis of many quick weeknight meals.

Makes 1¼ cups

½ cup **Sweet-sour syrup** (page 207)
1 tablespoon cornstarch
1 teaspoon sambal oelek chili garlic sauce*
½ cup soy sauce
¼ cup water
1 tablespoon lime juice
1 tablespoon fish sauce** (optional)
¼ cup roughly chopped, packed fresh ginger

1. Make **Sweet-sour syrup.**
2. Place ½ cup syrup, cornstarch, chili garlic sauce, soy sauce, and water together in a small saucepan. Whisk together and bring to a boil.
3. Lower heat and simmer, whisking constantly, for about 20 seconds. Remove from heat and stir in lime juice and fish sauce, if using.
4. Place mixture in a blender and add ginger. Blend on high speed for 10 seconds.

Sambal oelek is available in Asian markets or the Asian foods section of some grocery stores. The brand I use comes in an 8-ounce jar with a rooster on the front. For more information, see Resources: Asian Ingredients.

**Fish sauce, also known as nam pla, is available in Asian markets or the Asian foods section of some grocery stores. Look for Dragonfly or Golden Boy brands.*

continued⟶

Tilapia with pan-Asian ginger sauce

continued from previous page

Notes:

+ If you make extra sauce, use it in stir-fried dishes or add lime juice for a salad dressing or marinade for chicken, beef, fish, or tofu.
+ For a dipping sauce, simply omit the cornstarch and ginger, and do not cook. Serve with tempura, pot stickers, spring rolls, or dim sum.
+ Increase the amount of lime juice to make an oil-free salad dressing.

Cambodian coleslaw

This is another recipe inspired by our wonderful Cambodian cook, Pen Leng. The dressing's combination of hot, sour, salty, and sweet flavors accents the pure, fresh taste of the vegetables.

Serves 6 to 8

Sweet-sour dressing (recipe follows)
1 small head green cabbage (about ¾ pound)
1 small carrot, peeled and grated
2 green onions, thinly sliced on an angle
½ pound mung bean sprouts, rinsed and drained
½ cup chopped fresh cilantro
⅓ cup chopped fresh mint
½ cup chopped fresh basil

1. Make **Sweet-sour dressing.**
2. Cut cabbage in half and slice as thinly as you can. (A Japanese mandolin is perfect for this.) Place in a large mixing bowl with the reserved herb mixture; add the carrot, green onions, and sprouts. Toss with dressing no more than 15 minutes before serving.

> Notes:
> + You can add all sorts of vegetables to this salad, such as red pepper, jicama, and zucchini strips or cucumber. Finely minced red peppers can be sprinkled on top of the salad for a nice presentation.
> + We usually present this salad on a large platter surrounded by baby lettuces.
> + Serve this salad with meat, if desired: thinly slice leftover chicken, pork, or beef, coat lightly with dressing, and arrange around the salad.

Sweet-sour dressing

Makes 1¼ cups

⅓ cup roughly chopped fresh mint
½ cup roughly chopped fresh cilantro
½ cup roughly chopped fresh basil
1 tablespoon minced fresh garlic
½ cup lime juice
⅓ cup honey
½ fresh jalapeño pepper, with seeds, roughly chopped
2 teaspoons fish sauce (optional)*
2 tablespoons dry-roasted peanuts

continued⟶

Cambodian coleslaw

continued from previous page

1. Place all ingredients in a blender and blend on high speed until fairly smooth, about 6 seconds. A little texture is desirable; puréeing fresh herbs completely can "flatten out" the flavors.

* Fish sauce, also known as nam pla, is available in Asian markets or the Asian foods section of some grocery stores. Look for Dragonfly or Golden Boy brands.

Notes:
- Jalapeños vary in degree of spiciness. The amount called for in this recipe usually results in a medium-hot dressing. Start with less if your tolerance for chiles is limited.
- Fish sauce is optional, but I recommend it for authentic flavor. For a vegetarian dressing, omit the fish sauce and add 1 teaspoon kosher salt and 2 teaspoons soy sauce.
- Pen Leng often uses only cilantro when making this dressing. I like the fresh, varied flavor from using all three herbs. If you use only one herb, use cilantro.
- Try the dressing as a dipping sauce for spring rolls.
- To make a **Cambodian-style spicy shrimp**, toss 1 pound peeled and deveined medium shrimp (size 21 to 25) with ½ cup of the dressing and 1 teaspoon salt. Let sit 15 minutes, spread on an oiled cookie sheet in one layer, and bake at 350° for 3 to 5 minutes. Cool shrimp, toss with another ¼ cup of dressing, and serve.

Gingered ice cream
with sesame crisps

Everyone loves homemade ice cream, but finding time to make it can be a challenge. Here's a good compromise: purchase high-quality vanilla ice cream and fold in your favorite flavoring ingredients, then serve with a cookie or sauce. Remember to prepare the ice cream at least four hours before serving, so it has time to refreeze.

Serves 6 to 8

1 quart high-quality vanilla ice cream
6 ounces crystallized ginger, minced
Sesame crisps (recipe follows)

1. Soften ice cream: Either microwave in 10-second bursts, checking often, until ice cream is soft enough to stir with a wooden spoon, or simply set out at room temperature for about 15 minutes.
2. Stir in crystallized ginger, place in a plastic tub, and refreeze.
3. Serve ice cream with **Sesame crisps**.

Notes:
+ More ideas for your "home-flavored" ice cream: crumbled almond cookies (amaretti) or coconut macaroons; puréed fruit, such as raspberries or peaches; or caramelized nuts.
+ To create a marbled effect, swirl in flavorings such as fudge sauce or peanut butter after briefly softening them in the microwave. An equally attractive—and even easier—method of combining flavors can be achieved by mixing different ice creams right in the scoop: fill an ice cream scoop halfway with chocolate ice cream and finish with vanilla, for example.

Sesame crisps

Adapted from a Florentine cookie recipe, these lacy, caramelized crisps make an elegant garnish. They can also be shaped into cups or small cones (while still hot and soft), then cooled and filled with flavored whipped cream, chocolate ganache, or custard.

Makes 25 cookies

¼ cup sugar
¼ cup honey
¼ cup (½ stick) unsalted butter
¼ cup all-purpose flour, sifted
¼ cup sesame seeds

continued—>

Gingered ice cream
with sesame crisps

continued from previous page

1. Preheat oven to 350°. Place a sheet of parchment paper on a baking pan and coat the paper lightly with canola or salad oil.
2. In a small saucepan, heat sugar, honey, and butter over medium heat, stirring occasionally, until sugar is dissolved. Add flour and sesame seeds, and whisk until smooth.
3. Drop heaping teaspoonfuls of batter about 2 inches apart onto prepared pan.
4. Bake 6 to 8 minutes, until golden brown.

Notes:
+ Crisps can be baked directly on a lightly oiled baking pan; but they must be removed while still hot or they will adhere to the pan as they cool.
+ Batter can be made in the microwave: heat honey and butter until butter is completely melted. Mix in sugar and sesame seeds, then flour.
+ This recipe can be doubled or otherwise scaled up directly as much as needed, since it has equal amounts of every ingredient. The leftover batter will keep, refrigerated, for 2 weeks.
+ For a milder flavor, substitute light corn syrup for honey.
+ Many things can be used in place of the sesame seeds. Try roughly chopped pumpkinseeds, pecans, or roasted cocoa beans (also called cacao nibs); For more information go to www.scharffenberger.com (click on Shop Online, then Bulk Pro Packs). Remember to roughly chop any of these ingredients before adding them to the batter.

Valentine's Day Dinner

According to legend, a Roman named St. Valentine was thrown into prison and martyred for defying the emperor. He left a farewell note for the jailer's daughter, signed "from your Valentine." In his honor, we celebrate romance on this day. So gather your dearest friends, cook for them, and light the candles.

Carrot soup with ginger
and parsley cream

Angel hair pasta with shrimp,
red peppers, spinach, and
lemon-garlic sauce

Butter lettuce with grapefruit,
toasted almonds, and beet
vinaigrette

Chocolate beet-cake with
ganache and cinnamon
custard sauce

Carrot soup
with ginger and parsley cream

This savory purée comes alive with a good jolt of ginger, a bright orange color, and a cooling contrast of parsley cream.

Serves 6/Makes 2½ quarts

2 tablespoons canola or salad oil
1 medium onion, roughly chopped
¼ cup peeled, finely chopped, tightly packed ginger
2 pounds carrots (about 7 medium), peeled and thinly sliced
1 small potato (½ pound), peeled and roughly chopped
2 quarts water or chicken stock
Parsley cream (recipe follows)
½ cup whipping cream
2 teaspoons kosher salt
Pinch of white pepper

1. Heat oil in a medium stockpot over medium heat until it SHIMMERS. Add onion, ginger, and carrots. Cook over medium heat, stirring occasionally, 3 to 5 minutes, or until onions are translucent but not brown.
2. Add potato and water. Simmer, covered, 45 minutes to 1 hour, until ingredients are very soft.
3. Make **Parsley cream**; cover and refrigerate until serving time.
4. Purée soup in batches in a blender on high speed until very smooth, covering blender with a cloth to prevent hot mixture from spraying. Pour soup through a mesh strainer. Return soup to stockpot and add whipping cream, salt, and pepper.
5. Serve warm with a dollop of parsley cream.

   Note:
   + This soup can be served with a sprinkle of chopped parsley or **Easy garlic croutons** instead of the parsley cream.

Parsley cream

Makes 1¼ cups

1 cup sour cream
½ cup chopped Italian parsley leaves
1 tablespoon lemon juice
Pinch of white pepper (optional)
½ teaspoon kosher salt

1. Place all ingredients in a blender. Blend on high speed 10 seconds, or until smooth.

Angel hair pasta with shrimp, red peppers, spinach, and lemon-garlic sauce

Delicate angel hair pasta is perfect for Valentine's Day. This winning dish has a great combination of flavors, colors, and textures.

Serves 6

Lemon-garlic sauce (recipe follows)
1 tablespoon kosher salt
1 pound angel hair pasta
½ pound spinach, stemmed and roughly chopped
2 **roasted red peppers**, peeled, seeded, and thinly sliced (page 203)
½ cup thinly sliced fresh basil leaves
1 teaspoon black pepper
1½ pounds shrimp, peeled and deveined
6 fresh basil leaves for garnish

1. Make **Lemon-garlic sauce**. Assemble all other ingredients before cooking pasta.
2. Bring 3 quarts of water and the salt to a boil. Cook pasta for 3 minutes, or until just barely done. Do not overcook. Drain in a colander.
3. Place lemon-garlic sauce in a large pan over medium-high heat and bring to a boil. Add spinach, roasted peppers, sliced basil, and black pepper.
   Heat just until bubbles start to form and spinach is wilted.
4. Add shrimp and cook until they turn pink, about 2 to 3 minutes. Add pasta and heat through.
5. Serve immediately with a basil leaf on top of each serving.

   Notes:
   + Regular spinach is fine for this recipe, but baby spinach can be purchased already clean and does not require chopping.
   + Large "tail-on" shrimp are attractive but can be expensive; I find that size 21 to 25 shrimp are often the best value. Or try smaller rock shrimp, which are very juicy and are often available already peeled.
   + You can finish this recipe two ways: Start the lemon-garlic sauce reheating in the large pan and then cook the pasta. While the pasta is cooking, add the remaining ingredients to the sauce. Then add the drained pasta. With this method, care must be taken to avoid overcooking the pasta. Or cook the pasta ahead of time (undercook it a bit), drain, then rinse in cold water to stop the cooking. When you're ready to finish the dish, add drained pasta to the sauce with the rest of the ingredients as directed above. This method works well when you have other things cooking and you need some flexibility with the timing.

continued⟶

Angel hair pasta with shrimp, red peppers, spinach, and lemon-garlic sauce

continued from previous page

Lemon-garlic sauce

Makes 2 cups

2 tablespoons cornstarch
3 ounces lemon juice
¼ cup olive oil
¼ cup minced fresh garlic
2 cups dry white wine
¼ cup (½ stick) unsalted butter
2 teaspoons kosher salt
¼ teaspoon sugar

1. Whisk together cornstarch and lemon juice. Set aside.
2. In a medium saucepan over medium-high heat, heat olive oil until it SHIMMERS. Add garlic and cook, stirring, about 30 seconds, but do not brown. Add wine and boil for a minute to burn off the alcohol.
3. Whisk the lemon juice mixture into the boiling wine mixture and simmer for 30 seconds, whisking occasionally. Remove from heat and whisk in butter, salt, and sugar. Set aside.

Butter lettuce
with grapefruit, toasted almonds, and beet vinaigrette

This light salad cleanses the palate before a rich dessert. For a more complex salad, add raisins, jicama, sprouts, or shredded carrot.

Serves 6

1 large head butter lettuce, torn into small pieces
Beet vinaigrette (recipe follows)
2 grapefruits, peeled, seeded, and cut into sections
¼ cup sliced almonds, toasted

1. Place lettuce in a bowl and toss with enough beet vinaigrette to coat lightly.
2. Place dressed salad in a serving bowl or on plates, surround with grapefruit segments, and sprinkle with toasted almonds. Drizzle a little more vinaigrette around salad.

Beet vinaigrette

This deep-red dressing is rich, smooth, and creamy without the use of traditional thickeners, such as egg.

Makes 1½ cups

1 small red beet, cooked, peeled, and roughly chopped (about ½ cup)
2 tablespoons chopped red onion or shallot
¼ cup plus 1 tablespoon red wine vinegar
2 tablespoons water
1 teaspoon kosher salt
½ teaspoon black pepper
¾ cup good olive oil

1. Place the beet, onion, vinegar, water, salt, and pepper in a blender. Blend on high speed 8 to 10 seconds, until very smooth.
2. With the motor running, add oil in a thin stream until it is fully incorporated. (See EMULSIFY in Resources: Glossary.)

> Notes:
> + Using puréed vegetables to make creamy-style dressings is a great way to lighten up your salads.
> + To cook beets, boil them in their skin about 20 minutes; or place them in an oiled baking pan with ½ inch water, cover the pan with foil, and roast in a 400° oven about 45 minutes. Beets are done when a paring knife goes in easily. Roasting beets concentrates the flavors, whereas boiling them dilutes the flavors a bit. Cool before using in vinaigrette recipe.
> + This vinaigrette is a great way to use up leftover cooked beets.

Chocolate beet-cake
with chocolate ganache and cinnamon custard sauce

I have two requirements for a chocolate cake: it must be moist and very chocolaty. See if your friends can guess the "secret ingredient."

Makes 1 (9-inch round) single-layer cake

Cinnamon custard sauce (recipe follows)
1½ cups peeled and finely chopped raw red beets
2 tablespoons water
3 eggs
1 teaspoon vanilla extract
1 cup canola or salad oil
½ cup cocoa powder, preferably Dutch process
½ teaspoon baking soda
¼ teaspoon table salt
¾ cup plus 1 tablespoon sugar
¾ cup all-purpose flour
Chocolate ganache (recipe follows)

1. Make **Cinnamon custard sauce**.
2. Preheat oven to 350°. Oil and flour a 9-inch round cake pan.
3. Place beets, water, eggs, vanilla, and oil in a blender. Blend 10 to 15 seconds on high speed, until very smooth. Pour into a mixing bowl.
4. Sift together dry ingredients. Add to the bowl with beet-water mixture and stir with a rubber spatula just until combined. Pour into prepared pan. Batter will almost fill pan.
5. Bake 30 to 35 minutes, or until the center springs back when touched lightly and a skewer inserted in the middle comes out dry. Cool cake for 10 minutes in pan, then run a paring knife around the edge of pan and turn out onto a rack to cool completely.
6. Make **Chocolate ganache**.
7. The cake can be finished either as a layer cake or cut into "heart-beets," as described in step 8. For layer cake, cut cake in half horizontally. Spread half of ganache on the cut side of one cake round. Top with other cake round. Frost the top and sides with remaining ganache. Chill at least 30 minutes before cutting into wedges and serving.
8. For heart-beets, use deep heart-shape cutters (available from party supply stores and some grocery stores) to cut cake into heart-shaped pieces. Refrigerate ganache, stirring occasionally, until it is the consistency of yogurt, then quickly spoon into a pastry bag fitted with a star tip. Pipe a "kiss" of ganache onto each heart-beet by holding the pastry bag straight above it, squeezing a dollop on top, then lifting the pastry bag straight up. To garnish heart-beets, press a whole toasted almond into each kiss of ganache.

    Notes:
    + When baked and cooled, this cake is a little more than an inch high. For an impressively high two-layer cake, double the cake recipe, bake in two cake pans, and use the ganache to hold the two cakes together and frost the top.
    + The cake can be wrapped in plastic and refrigerated for up to 4 days, or frozen for up to a month.

Chocolate ganache

¾ cup whipping cream
1 cup finely chopped bittersweet chocolate
2 tablespoons rum or brandy

1. Bring cream just to a boil in a small saucepan, then remove from heat. Add chocolate and let sit for 5 minutes.
2. Whisk together until very smooth. Drizzle in rum while whisking.

   Notes:
   + Pastry bags are available in specialty kitchen supply stores, along with star tips, which add decorative grooves to whatever you're piping. With just the star tip, you can make a serviceable pastry bag out of a zip-top bag: cut a small corner off the bag and put the star tip inside (in the corner of the bag) with the small end of the tip poking out. Spoon your ganache into the bag and proceed.
   + Ganache can be used to make chocolate truffles. Mix 3 tablespoons each cocoa and powdered sugar on a plate. Use a pastry bag with a plain tip to pipe gumball-sized spheres of ganache directly onto the plate. Gently roll the ganache to coat all sides. Move chocolate truffles to another plate and refrigerate until firm.

Cinnamon custard sauce

Makes 2 cups

1. Prepare **Custard sauce** (page 198) as directed, and stir in 1 teaspoon ground cinnamon with vanilla in step 4.

Carnaval Celebration

This menu was inspired by a wonderful trip I took to Brazil. I visited a friend in the northeastern town of Salvador, in the state of Bahia, and we celebrated Carnaval for almost a week—along with a few million other people! When I came home, I threw a party at Westerbeke Ranch so I could share the experience in my favorite way: through food and drink. This menu is based on the one I served.

Chicken and shrimp stew

Potato and onion gratin
with coconut milk

Cornmeal-crusted eggplant

Green salad with mango,
red pepper, jicama, red onion,
and mango vinaigrette

Frozen dulce de leche parfait
with cashew-chocolate sauce

Chicken and shrimp stew

This recipe is called Xinxim (pronounced "sheen sheem") in Portuguese. It features ingredients that are plentiful in Brazil: coconuts, peanuts, and shrimp. It's kind of like a tropical version of chicken cacciatore. Although the ingredient list is long, the technique is simple and the result is well worth the time.

Serves 8 to 10

2 (3-pound) chickens, each cut into 8 pieces
1 teaspoon black pepper
2½ teaspoons kosher salt, divided
⅓ cup canola or salad oil
1 small white onion, diced
4 stalks celery, diced
1 small green pepper, diced
1 tablespoon plus 1 teaspoon minced fresh garlic
2 tablespoons peeled, minced fresh ginger
⅓ cup roasted salted peanuts
2 cups chicken stock, vegetable stock, or water
1½ cups canned diced tomatoes in their juice
1 tablespoon shrimp powder* or ground dried shrimp
1 (13½-ounce) can unsweetened coconut milk
½ pound uncooked medium shrimp (size 21 to 25), peeled and deveined
½ teaspoon red chile flakes or ¼ teaspoon cayenne pepper (optional)
1 tablespoon lime juice

1. Coat chicken well with pepper and 2 teaspoons of the salt. Set aside while you assemble and measure the other ingredients.
2. In a large pan (at least 12 inches in diameter) over medium-high heat, heat the oil until it SHIMMERS. Add chicken pieces and brown on all sides (in two batches if necessary). Remove chicken and discard the oil. In the same pan over medium heat, add onion, celery, green pepper, garlic, and ginger. Cook until the onions are translucent, scraping the pan to incorporate the browned bits.
3. Place the peanuts and stock in a blender. Blend on high speed for 15 seconds, or until smooth and add to pan.
4. Add tomatoes, shrimp powder, and coconut milk.
   Simmer, covered, for 30 minutes or until chicken is very tender, stirring occasionally.
5. Remove from heat and add the shrimp, chile flakes, lime juice, and remaining ½ teaspoon salt. Stir and let sit a few minutes to cook shrimp.

Shrimp powder is available in Latin markets or the Mexican food section of large supermarkets. It is a great flavor booster for shrimp dishes and can be used in many recipes, including Asian soups and sauces, and Louisiana-style dishes such as jambalaya.

Notes:

- Large "tail-on" shrimp are attractive but can be expensive; I find that size 21 to 25 are often the best value. Or try smaller rock shrimp, which are very juicy and are often available already peeled.
- This dish can be served with white rice.
- This dish is often made with both peanuts and cashews, which are a huge crop in Brazil. I simplified the stew somewhat and removed the cashews. However, they do make a nice garnish: if desired, sprinkle ⅓ cup roasted salted cashews on top when serving.

Potato and onion gratin
with coconut milk

Coconut milk makes this a rich and satisfying dish without any cream or dairy products. The gratin is simple to make and goes well with a surprising number of entrées; try it with pork, beef, or your favorite vegetarian entrée.

Serves 8

4 medium russet potatoes (about 2½ pounds total)
1 small yellow or white onion
2½ teaspoons kosher salt
¾ teaspoon black pepper
¼ cup water
1 (13½-ounce) can unsweetened coconut milk*

1. Preheat oven to 375°.
2. Peel potatoes and onion, and slice thinly. Place in a large bowl and add the salt, pepper, water, and coconut milk. Toss well to coat completely. Oil an 8 by 8 by 2-inch baking pan. Pack the potato mixture into the pan and cover with a lightly oiled piece of foil, oiled side down.
3. Bake 1½ hours. Remove foil and cool 10 minutes before serving.

Notes:
+ For individual plate presentations, make this dish a day ahead. After baking, press a pan of the same size onto the top of foil to flatten gratin and push out any air bubbles. Refrigerate overnight. Remove foil, pass the pan briefly over a gas flame to loosen gratin, run a paring knife around the edge of the pan, and turn out gratin. Cut into squares or triangles. Arrange portions on an oiled baking pan and warm in a 375° oven 8 minutes, or until heated through.
+ As a variation on this recipe, try half potatoes and half yams.

* Unsweetened coconut milk can be found in Asian markets or the Asian foods section of some grocery stores. Look for Chaokoh or 7 Lotus brands.

Cornmeal-crusted eggplant

Farofa, or cassava meal, is frequently served as a side dish in Brazil. Farofa is a bit of an acquired taste and not commonly available in this country, so I created a dish that uses cornmeal in its place. A little spicy, a little sweet, and pleasantly grainy, this dish complements foods with a creamy texture.

Serves 8

8 Japanese eggplants, ends removed
Cornmeal crust (recipe follows)
½ teaspoon kosher salt
½ cup canola or salad oil

1. Slice eggplants in half lengthwise. Place in a large mixing bowl and sprinkle with salt. Toss well to coat completely. Let sit for 10 minutes.
2. Make **Cornmeal crust**. Dredge eggplant halves in crust, pressing cut side down to coat. Lightly shake off excess. Lay eggplants on a baking pan.
3. In a large sauté pan over medium-high heat, heat oil until it SHIMMERS. Lay eggplant in oil, cut side down, and cook until brown. Reduce heat to medium, turn eggplants over, and cook skin side until soft. Drain eggplants on paper towels to blot excess oil.
4. Serve immediately, or set aside on a baking pan and reheat 5 minutes in a preheated 350° oven.

   Notes:
   + You can also use regular eggplant for this recipe: Cut 1 large eggplant into ½-inch-thick round slices. Proceed as above, but press both sides of eggplant rounds into cornmeal.
   + For a Creole-style dish, top with a dollop of **caramelized onions** mixed with a little apple cider vinegar and a pinch of sugar.

Cornmeal crust

Try this crust for fried green tomatoes, tilapia, or catfish.

Makes 1 cup

¾ cup cornmeal
1 tablespoon onion powder
1 tablespoon granulated garlic
¼ teaspoon cayenne pepper
1½ teaspoons black pepper
1 teaspoon kosher salt
1½ teaspoons sugar

1. Grind the cornmeal 5 seconds in an electric spice or coffee mill.
2. Add cornmeal to remaining ingredients and stir to combine.

Green salad with mango,
red pepper, jicama, red onion, and mango vinaigrette

Many Central and South American countries don't have a salad course per se. But a meal at Westerbeke Ranch without a salad? Not on my watch.

Serves 8

¾ pound mixed greens (mesclun mix, baby spinach, or your favorite)
Mango vinaigrette (recipe follows)
1 ripe mango, peeled, pitted, and cut into ¼-inch cubes
½ small jicama, peeled and thinly sliced
1 red bell pepper, thinly sliced
⅓ cup thinly sliced red onion

1. Place greens in a large bowl and toss with **Mango vinaigrette** until lightly coated.
2. Arrange mango and jicama around salad. Sprinkle red pepper and red onion on top.

   Notes:
   + Ripe papaya can be substituted for the mango.
   + I prefer to use **Roasted red peppers** for this recipe (see Essential Recipes).
   + Hearts of palm also go well with this salad, as well as roasted salted cashews.

Mango vinaigrette

Makes 1½ cups

1 ripe mango, peeled
Small pinch cayenne pepper
¼ cup plus 2 tablespoons seasoned rice wine vinegar
Juice of 1 lime (about 2 tablespoons)
1 teaspoon kosher salt
¼ teaspoon white pepper (optional)
¼ cup plus 1 tablespoon water
¼ cup canola or salad oil

1. Remove all of the mango from the pit and chop the fruit roughly. Place 1 cup of the mango in a blender and add cayenne, vinegar, lime juice, salt, pepper, and water. Blend on high speed for 8 seconds, or until smooth.
2. Remove top of blender and, with motor running, slowly pour in oil. Vinaigrette will thicken as it sits. Thin with a little water if necessary.

   Notes:
   + Add any remaining mango to the salad.
   + This dressing can be used as a light sauce for fish. Try sprinkling a halibut steak with Madras curry powder and kosher salt, grilling or broiling, and serving with vinaigrette.

Frozen dulce de leche parfaits
with cashew-chocolate sauce

Dulce de leche (Spanish for "sweet with milk") is enjoyed throughout Latin America, where cooks boil sweetened condensed milk—right in the can! In this frozen version, you'll be surprised at the smooth texture you can achieve without the hassle of making ice cream.

Serves 8 to 10/Makes about 2 quarts

1 (14-ounce) can sweetened condensed milk, preferably organic
2 cups whipping cream
1 teaspoon vanilla extract
4 eggs
¼ cup water
Cashew-chocolate sauce (recipe follows)

1. Preheat oven to 425°. Pour sweetened condensed milk into an 8-inch glass pie plate. Cover with foil and place in a shallow pan. fill pan with hot water. Bake one hour or until milk is thick and caramel colored. Transfer to a large mixing bowl.
2. Whip cream and vanilla to soft-peak stage, then set aside.
3. Pour about ¾ inch water in the bottom of a double boiler, making certain top pan will not touch water. Bring water to a boil, then reduce heat to simmer. Crack eggs into the top of double boiler and add the ¼ cup water. Place the bowl over the saucepan and whisk mixture by hand until it is very fluffy and hot to the touch (145° on an instant-read thermometer, if you have one). You now have a French sabayon (or, in Italian, zabaglione). Remove from heat and beat with an electric mixer on medium-high speed until cool and ribbony, about 6 minutes.
4. Add half the sabayon to the caramelized condensed milk and whisk until the mixture is completely smooth. Use a rubber spatula to fold in the remaining sabayon.
   Fold in the whipped cream.
5. Line an 8 x 8 x 2-inch baking pan with plastic wrap and pour the mixture into it. Cover with plastic wrap and freeze for at least 4 hours, or overnight.
6. Make **Cashew-chocolate sauce** and set aside.
7. To serve, remove plastic wrap from top of baking pan. Invert pan onto a clean cutting board. Remove plastic, cut into rectangles, and place on dessert plates. Spoon some of the cashew-chocolate sauce around the parfaits.

   Notes:
   + Individual servings are pretty with either a dollop of whipped cream and a mint leaf, or a little cookie inserted into the top.
   + Try freezing the parfait in different shapes, such as a round cake pan, loaf pans, or even muffin tins (which will freeze much faster than a larger pan). If your pans or muffin tins are very clean, you can omit the plastic wrap and dip the bottom of the frozen pan briefly in hot water to unmold the parfait.
   + The yield of 2 quarts may sound like a lot, but this is a very airy dessert. Also, what you don't use can be frozen for up to a month.

continued——→

Frozen dulce de leche parfait
with cashew-chocolate sauce

continued from previous page

Cashew-chocolate sauce

Chocolate sauces often contain cream. Here, I've substituted a smooth cashew purée, which gives the sauce a rich texture without masking the deep flavor of chocolate.

Makes 1½ cups

½ cup roasted unsalted cashews
1½ cups water
¼ teaspoon kosher salt
¾ cup finely chopped high-quality bittersweet chocolate
¼ cup sugar
½ teaspoon vanilla extract

1. Bring cashews, water, and salt to a boil in a small saucepan. Remove from heat and add chocolate and sugar. Cover immediately and let sit 15 minutes.
2. Place mixture in a blender, add vanilla, and blend on high speed 30 seconds, or until completely smooth.

> Notes:
> + Look for Scharffen Berger, Valrhona, Callebaut, or Guittard chocolate.
> + Like any chocolate sauce, this one goes well with ice cream, frozen confections such as Soy Dream, and sundaes, cakes, brownies, and cookies.
> + For coconut-chocolate sauce, replace the cashews and water with a (13½-ounce) can of coconut milk.

Vegetarian Entrées

Vegetarian Entrées

In this section, vegetarians and curious omnivores can find options to replace meat, poultry, and fish entrées in this book. Most of the vegetarian recipes are building blocks you can use to create other dishes.

Every group that visits Westerbeke Ranch sends us a list of dietary requirements before arriving. Most groups have at least a few vegetarians. Some groups request entirely vegetarian menus. Since our guests often stay for up to a week at a time, my repertoire of vegetarian dishes has greatly expanded since I started cooking at the Ranch.

To please both vegetarians and meat eaters, I often begin cooking a meatless dish, then split it into two versions, one with meat and one without. For example, if I'm cooking a shrimp jambalaya, I will sauté the onion, bell pepper, celery, and garlic until they start to soften, then add some white wine and simmer a few minutes, then add tomatoes and seasonings. I will split this "base" into two batches: to one, I will add vegetable stock and then, near the end, some crispy tofu cubes. The other batch will get fish stock, then, near the end, some shrimp. Both batches will be served with rice and other side dishes.

Butternut squash curry

Cashew-crusted tofu with gingered butternut squash sauce

Corn chip–crusted tofu with fresh tomato salsa

Mushroom stroganoff

Stuffed portobello mushrooms with cashew "cream" sauce

Vegan Caesar salad

Vegetarian chili

Butternut squash curry

Butternut squash, with a color and flavor somewhat like pumpkin, can be incorporated into soups, sauces, pasta dishes, gratins, or stews. Here is one of my favorite ways to prepare this winter squash.

Serves 8 to 10/Makes 9 cups

¼ cup canola oil
1 cup chopped yellow onion (about 1 small)
1 cup chopped celery (about 3 stalks)
2 tablespoons minced fresh garlic
2 tablespoons Madras curry powder
1 cup dry white wine or water
2 cups vegetable stock*
7 cups peeled butternut squash, cut into ¾-inch cubes (about a 3-pound squash)
1 (14-ounce) can unsweetened coconut milk
2 tablespoons cornstarch
2 tablespoons cold water
2 teaspoons kosher salt
2 teaspoons lemon juice
¼ cup chopped green onion

1. In a large saucepan or small stockpot over medium heat, heat oil until it SHIMMERS. Add onion, celery, and garlic and cook, stirring, until onion is translucent. Add curry powder and cook, stirring, about 10 seconds or until very fragrant. Add wine, cook a few minutes to burn off alcohol, then add stock and squash. Bring to a boil, reduce to simmer, and cook, covered, 12 to 15 minutes, until squash is soft but not falling apart.
2. Add coconut milk. Mix cornstarch and water and stir in, bring back to a boil, and simmer about 20 seconds until thickened. Stir in salt and lemon juice and serve immediately, with chopped green onion for garnish.

As a quick substitute for vegetable stock, try vegetarian chicken broth mix, available in the bulk foods section of natural foods stores. Whisk in 1 tablespoon for each cup of hot water.

Notes:
+ Serve with plain white rice or **Jasmine rice–quinoa pilaf** and mango chutney.
+ Freeze any extra curry in plastic zip-top bags for up to a month.
+ Tofu can be added to the curry: use 1 (14-ounce) block, cut into ½-inch cubes. Dry tofu in a few changes of paper towels, then add with the coconut milk. To make tofu more sturdy, bake cubes on an oiled baking pan in a preheated 325° oven for 20 minutes before adding to curry. This will produce a "skin" on tofu cubes.
+ Here are a few delicious additions:
    1 tablespoon yellow or brown mustard seeds (add with squash)
    2½ cups canned diced tomatoes with juice (add with coconut milk)
    2 tablespoons minced fresh ginger (add with squash)

Cashew-crusted tofu
with gingered butternut squash sauce

This recipe and the one that follows utilize a method I use often: slice the tofu into "cutlet" shapes, coat it with a crust, sauté, and serve with a sauce. This creates a full-flavored and satisfying vegetarian entrée.

Serves 4 to 6

1 (14-ounce) package extra-firm tofu
2 teaspoons kosher salt, divided
Cashew crust (recipe follows)
¼ cup flour or cornstarch
½ cup milk or soy milk
¼ cup canola or salad oil
Gingered butternut squash sauce (recipe follows)

1. Drain tofu well. Wrap in a double layer of paper towels and press out as much moisture as possible. Discard paper towels and slice tofu block into 8 slices (as you would a loaf of bread). Lay another piece of paper towel on work surface, sprinkle with 1 teaspoon salt, then lay tofu slices on salted paper towel. Sprinkle another teaspoon salt on top of tofu and cover with another piece of paper towel. Press down on paper towels (or set a baking sheet on top of paper towel–covered tofu to exert even pressure) for 10 seconds or so to remove as much moisture as possible.
2. Make **Cashew crust** and place in a bowl.
3. Set up a "breading station": place flour in a medium bowl and milk in another bowl. Arrange flour, milk, and cashew crust in a row on work surface. Place the dried tofu slices to the left of the flour and begin breading: dredge slices in flour, covering completely. Lightly shake off excess flour, and dredge in milk and cashew crust. Place "breaded" tofu on a baking sheet. Repeat this process until all the tofu is coated.
4. In a large sauté pan over medium heat, heat oil until it SHIMMERS. Carefully lay one piece of coated tofu in the pan to test heat. Tofu should bubble vigorously. Fry 4 pieces at a time. Brown both sides, then remove to paper towels and blot excess oil. Serve with the butternut squash sauce.

Cashew crust

Makes about 1¼ cups

¾ cup panko or plain bread crumbs
½ cup unsalted raw or roasted cashews
½ teaspoon kosher salt

1. Place all ingredients in a food processor. Process 30 seconds, or until mixture resembles cornmeal.

continued——➔

Cashew-crusted tofu
with gingered butternut squash sauce

continued from previous page

Gingered butternut squash sauce

Makes 2 cups

2½ cups peeled and diced butternut squash
1½ cups vegetable stock
2 tablespoons minced fresh ginger
2 teaspoons minced fresh garlic
Salt to taste

1. Place all ingredients in a medium saucepan and bring to a boil. Reduce heat and simmer, covered, 15 minutes or until squash is very soft. Blend on high speed in a blender for 6 seconds, until very smooth. Taste and add salt if desired.

   Notes:
   + Some ideas for crispy tofu and sauce combinations: almond, hazelnut, or sunflower seed crust with **Mushroom gravy**; sesame crust with **Teriyaki sauce**; Italian herb crust with Spicy marinara sauce (add Parmesan cheese to the crust, melt a slice of mozzarella cheese on top, serve with **Spicy marinara sauce**, and you have tofu Parmesan); curry crust with mango chutney.
   + Some hints for creating your own crusts: When making nut crusts in the food processor, use about one part cornstarch or flour to three parts nuts. Processing pure nuts will result in nut butter, due to their high oil content. When making a Parmesan crust, use no more than one part cheese to two parts bread crumbs. Too much cheese will burn when sautéeing. A simple curry crust can be made with just curry powder, a dash of salt, and cornstarch or flour.

Corn chip–crusted tofu
with fresh tomato salsa

This variation on the "crispy cutlet" theme incorporates some of the best elements of Mexican cookery: corn and fresh tomatoes, chiles, cilantro, and lime juice.

Serves 4

Fresh tomato salsa (recipe follows)
1 (14-ounce) package extra-firm tofu
2 teaspoons kosher salt, divided
1 cup crushed corn chips
¼ cup flour or cornstarch
½ cup milk or soy milk
¼ cup canola or salad oil

1. Make **Fresh tomato salsa.**
2. Drain tofu well. Wrap in a double layer of paper towels and press out as much moisture as possible. Discard paper towels and slice tofu block into 8 slices (as you would a loaf of bread). Lay another piece of paper towel on work surface, sprinkle with 1 teaspoon salt, then lay tofu slices on salted paper towel. Sprinkle another teaspoon salt on top of tofu and cover with another piece of paper towel. Press down on paper towels (or set a baking sheet on top of paper towel–covered tofu to exert even pressure) for 10 seconds or so to remove as much moisture as possible.
3. Place corn chips in a food processor fitted with blade. Process 10 to 15 seconds, until mixture resembles cornmeal. Place in a medium bowl.
4. Set up a "breading station": place flour in a medium bowl and milk in another bowl. Arrange flour, milk, and corn chip crust in a row on work surface. Place the dried tofu slices to the left of the flour and begin breading: dredge slices in flour, covering completely. Lightly shake off excess flour, and dredge in milk and corn chip crust. Place "breaded" tofu on a baking sheet. Repeat this process until all the tofu is coated.
5. In a large sauté pan over medium-high heat, heat oil until it SHIMMERS. Lay one piece of coated tofu in the pan to test heat. Tofu should bubble vigorously. Fry 4 pieces at a time, brown on both sides, then remove to paper towels to blot excess oil. Serve with the salsa.

continued⟶

Corn chip–crusted tofu
with fresh tomato salsa

continued from previous page

Fresh tomato salsa

This is the basic "salsa fresca" made innumerable times every day in Mexico and the United States.

Makes about 2 cups

1½ cups diced fresh Roma tomatoes (about 3)
Scant ½ cup chopped cilantro (about ½ bunch)
1 to 2 tablespoons seeded, minced jalapeño chiles (1 to 1½ large)
¼ cup lime juice (from 2 limes)
1 teaspoon kosher salt
½ teaspoon black pepper
1 tablespoon orange juice
¼ cup minced red onion

1. Mix ingredients well, cover, and let sit at least 15 minutes. Increase chile and salt, if desired.

   Notes:
   + Roma tomatoes are commonly used because of their year-round availability, but this salsa is even better when prepared with vine-ripened summer tomatoes. It is even prettier when different-colored tomatoes are used.
   + If you like spicier foods, leave the seeds in when mincing the jalapeños.
   + Salsa fresca has as many versions as there are cooks. Some ideas: Substitute mangoes or ripe melons for the tomatoes, or mix tomatoes and diced melons or avocado. Pulse salsa in food processor until it's a chunky purée. Add minced zest of 1 lime. Add ½ cup **Three chile purée**. Add 1 tablespoon **Chipotle purée**. Using the amounts listed above, make a roasted tomato salsa: roughly chop tomatoes and onions, place in a bowl with stemmed whole jalapeño chile, lightly coat all with 1 tablespoon canola or salad oil, lay out on a baking pan and roast at 375° for 15 minutes or until blackened. Cool 10 minutes and place this mixture in a food processor. PULSE to a chunky purée stage (see Resources: Glossary).

Mushroom stroganoff

A hearty stew that puts the mushrooms center stage, this dish is great served with plain white rice or buttered noodles and a sprinkle of chopped parsley or green onions. The addition of dill pickles to a beef stroganoff is a tasty trick I learned from a fellow student in cooking school, and I've kept it in this vegetarian version. The gravy recipe makes more than you will need for the stroganoff, so you can stash some in the freezer for next time.

Serves 4/Makes 3 cups

1½ cups **Mushroom gravy** (recipe follows)
2 tablespoons olive oil
1 cup packed finely diced onion
¾ pound quartered cremini, or brown, mushrooms (about 1 quart packed)
1 cup dry white wine
2 tablespoons minced fresh garlic
2 tablespoons minced dill pickle
½ teaspoon kosher salt
2 teaspoons red wine vinegar

1. Make **Mushroom gravy.**
2. In a medium saucepan over medium-high heat, heat oil until it Shimmers, then add onion and mushrooms. Cook and stir until onion is translucent, 3 to 5 minutes. Add wine and garlic; simmer 5 minutes or until mushrooms and onion are tender. Add gravy, pickle, salt, and vinegar. Heat through and serve.

Notes:
  + For added protein add ½ block (7 ounces) extra-firm tofu, cut into ¾-inch cubes, when adding gravy.
  + To make this dish more like the original stroganoff, mix in ½ cup sour cream or **Cashew "cream" sauce** just before serving.

continued——➤

Mushroom stroganoff

continued from previous page

Mushroom gravy

This is a thick, rich sauce I developed to use in place of a strong-flavored meat-based brown sauce.

Makes about 9 cups

2 tablespoons canola or olive oil
1½ cups chopped onion (about 1 medium)
1 cup peeled, finely chopped carrots (about 1 medium)
2 stalks celery, chopped
1 quart water
1 cup canned diced tomatoes with their juice
10 cloves garlic
¾ pound quartered cremini, or brown, mushrooms (about 1 quart packed)
1 small or medium russet potato, peeled and chopped
1 cup dry red wine
⅓ cup soy sauce
2 teaspoons kosher salt

1. In medium saucepan over medium-high heat, heat oil until it SHIMMERS. Sauté onion, carrot, and celery a few minutes, until onion is translucent. Add water, tomatoes, garlic, mushrooms, and potato. Bring to a boil, reduce heat to a simmer, cover, and cook 45 minutes.
2. Add red wine; simmer, uncovered, 5 minutes to burn off alcohol. Remove from heat and add soy sauce and salt. Purée in batches in a blender on high speed for about 15 seconds, until very smooth, covering blender with lid and a cloth to prevent hot mixture from spraying.

Notes:
+ Serve gravy with stuffed portobellos, crispy tofu cutlets, or vegetable ravioli. Try truffle oil drizzled on top for an elegant finish. Thin gravy with vegetable stock, add some sautéed mushrooms and fresh herbs, and this sauce becomes a soup. Pour soup into bowls and top with some **Easy garlic croutons** and/or **Parsley cream**.
+ Creminis, also known as brown or Italian field mushrooms, contribute an earthy flavor to this sauce. For ultimate mushroom flavor, soak ⅛ ounce dried porcini mushrooms in 1 cup hot water for a few minutes, stir well, and lift mushrooms out of the water (leaving any dirt or grit at the bottom of container); add mushrooms to sauce with water and tomatoes.
+ Fresh herbs are a great addition to this sauce, especially thyme or marjoram.
+ Canned diced tomatoes can be replaced with 2 chopped fresh Roma tomatoes, or ¾ cup tomato sauce.

Stuffed portobello mushrooms
with cashew "cream" sauce

Roasted or grilled portobello mushrooms are the closest thing I know to a "vegetarian steak." Once you slice and roast the mushrooms, they can be stuffed with a wide variety of fillings, adding even more flavor. This is one vegetarian dish that can truly stand up to a big red wine!

Serves 6 (1 portobello per person)

1 tablespoon minced fresh garlic
¼ cup soy sauce
1 teaspoon sambal oelek chili sauce*
¼ cup canola or light olive oil
¼ cup dry white wine or water
6 medium-large portobello mushrooms
Fillings (suggestions follow)
Cashew or **Garlic cashew "cream" sauce** (recipes follow)

1. Preheat oven to 400°.
2. Mix garlic, soy sauce, chile sauce, oil, and wine in a medium mixing bowl. Remove and discard mushroom stems. Cut mushrooms horizontally into two slices—a sharp serrated knife works well for this—and dip each piece into the sauce. Place mushroom slices on an oiled baking sheet.
3. Bake 10 to 12 minutes.
4. When mushrooms are cool enough to handle, layer slices with **Fillings** of choice and reheat 6 to 8 minutes, or until heated through.
5. Serve with **Cashew**, or **Garlic cashew "cream" sauce.**

Cashew "cream" sauce

Makes about 2¾ cups

1 cup toasted unsalted cashews
2 cups water
1 teaspoon kosher salt

1. Bring nuts and water to a boil in a medium saucepan. Remove pan from heat, cover, and let sit 10 to 20 minutes.
2. Place cashew mixture and salt in a blender. Blend on high speed 2 to 3 minutes, or until nuts are completely smooth.

continued——>

Stuffed portobello mushrooms
with cashew "cream" sauce

continued from previous page

Garlic cashew "cream" sauce
This variation is for garlic lovers.

Makes about 2¾ cups

¾ cup vegetable stock
1 cup **Braised garlic** (page 194)
1 teaspoon kosher salt
Pinch of cayenne pepper
2 teaspoons seasoned rice wine vinegar
1 teaspoon minced fresh garlic
1 cup **Cashew "cream" sauce** (see preceding recipe)

1. Place stock, braised garlic, salt, cayenne, rice wine vinegar, and minced garlic in a blender and blend on high speed 5 seconds, until smooth.
2. Add **Cashew "cream" sauce** to blender and mix well.

   Note:
   + I often make a quick version of this sauce by substituting one cup whipping cream for the **Cashew "cream" sauce**. I call this **Braised garlic cream**.

Fillings:
Braised chard with browned garlic (1 bunch chard leaves will cook down to 1¼ cups, enough for a thin layer on 6 mushrooms), page 91
Jasmine rice–quinoa pilaf, page 49, or plain white rice
Buttermilk mashed potatoes, page 8
Roasted tomatoes (top each mushroom with a tomato half), page 204
Roasted butternut squash
Roasted red onion slices
Roasted eggplant slices
Raw, baked, smoked, or spice-rubbed tofu
Cooked and mashed black or pinto beans, soybeans, or chickpeas

   Note:
   + Stuffed portobellos go well with many other sauces, including **Spicy marinara sauce**, **Gingered butternut squash sauce**, **Mushroom gravy**, and pesto-cream sauce.

Sambal oelek is available in Asian markets or the Asian foods section of some grocery stores. The brand I use comes in an 8-ounce jar with a rooster on the front. For more information, see Resources, Asian Ingredients.

Vegan Caesar salad

A Caesar dressing without cheese, egg, and anchovies? My version substitutes creamy braised garlic for the egg and delivers the pungency of fresh garlic and the pucker of lemon juice.

Serves 6/1½ cups dressing

1 tablespoon minced fresh garlic
½ cup **Braised garlic** (page 194)
2 teaspoons vegetarian Worchestershire sauce*
3 tablespoons red wine vinegar
2 tablespoons lemon juice
1½ teaspoons kosher salt
½ teaspoon black pepper
¾ cup good olive oil
3 hearts of romaine lettuce
1 cup **Easy garlic croutons** (page 199)

1. Place first 7 ingredients in a blender or food processor. Blend until smooth, about 10 seconds. With the motor running, add oil in a thin stream until it is fully incorporated. (See Emulsify in Resources: Glossary.)
2. Taste for lemon juice, garlic, and salt, and increase if desired.
3. Cut each romaine heart in half lengthwise, keeping core attached. Slice into ¾-inch chunks. Discard core.
4. Toss lettuce and croutons with enough dressing to coat well.

Available in natural foods stores.

Notes:
+ An equal amount of silken tofu can be used in place of the braised garlic. Fresh garlic may need to be increased.
+ A Caesar is one of the few salads that's best a little overdressed.
+ Although not really an entrée, this salad can be the focus of a lunch or light dinner. Add sliced roasted portobello mushrooms or sautéed tofu cutlets for protein.

Vegetarian chili

This is a richly flavored chili that can be served for lunch or dinner, with any number of side dishes or salads. Don't forget the warm tortillas, cornbread, quesadillas, crackers, or garlic bread.

Serves 8 to 10/Makes 3½ quarts

¼ cup canola or salad oil
1 cup diced celery
2 cups diced onion
2 cups diced poblano chiles
2 cups diced bell pepper
¼ cup minced fresh garlic
4 tablespoons light chili powder
2 teaspoons granulated garlic
2 tablespoons granulated onion
2 teaspoons ground cumin
1 tablespoon ground coriander
1 cup vegetable stock*
¾ cup strong coffee
2 cups tomato juice
1 (28-ounce) can diced tomatoes with their juice
1 (28-ounce) can red kidney beans, drained
1 (28-ounce) can pinto or black beans, drained
1 tablespoon kosher salt
2 teaspoons black pepper

Garnishes:
Chopped red or green onion
Grated cheddar cheese
Sour cream
Chopped cilantro
Lime wedges
Tamari-roasted pumpkinseeds (page 208) or sunflower seeds

1. In a medium stockpot over high heat, heat oil until it SHIMMERS. Add celery, onion, chiles, and bell pepper, and cook, stirring frequently, about 8 minutes, or until onion is translucent.
2. Add fresh garlic and chili powder, granulated garlic, granulated onion, cumin, and coriander. Cook and stir for 2 minutes, until spices are very fragrant.
3. Stir in stock, coffee, tomato juice, tomatoes, and beans; cover, reduce heat, and simmer 25 minutes, stirring occasionally.
4. Stir in salt and pepper. Serve with desired garnishes.

* As a quick substitute for vegetable stock, try vegetarian chicken broth mix, available in the bulk foods section of natural foods stores. Whisk in 1 tablespoon for each cup of hot water.

Notes:
+ This is a medium-hot recipe, due to the chili powder. If you prefer less heat, start with 2 tablespoons chili powder and add more as desired at the end of cooking.
+ Try adding tofu: 1 (14-ounce) package firm or extra-firm tofu, drained well and cut into ¾-inch cubes. For a meat-like texture, freeze tofu overnight, thaw, squeeze dry, and cube, or process dried tofu briefly in food processor for a ground beef–like consistency.
+ Try adding vegetables: 2 zucchini, cubed; 1 (15½-ounce) can garbanzo beans, drained; 2 to 3 cups cubed butternut squash (add during the last 10 minutes of cooking); 1 large bunch of chopped leafy greens such as kale, spinach, or chard (add during the last 5 minutes of cooking).

Essential Recipes

This section contains recipes so dependable and versatile, they deserve their own chapter. I'm sure you will find them as indispensable as I do!

All-purpose brine
Balsamic vinegar reduction
Braised garlic
Caramelized onions
Chipotle barbecue sauce
Chipotle purée
Custard sauce
Easy garlic croutons
Pastry cream
Quick pizza sauce
Raspberry sauce
Roasted red peppers
Roasted tomatoes
Spicy marinara sauce
Sweetened whipped cream
Sweet-sour syrup
Tamari-roasted pumpkinseeds
Teriyaki sauce
Three chile purée

All-purpose brine

My friend and fellow chef Todd Muir shared this versatile recipe with me. I use it when I'm going to smoke salmon or roast pork, turkey, or whole chickens. The spices add subtle flavor, but all you really need are the salt, sugar, and water. Correctly brined meat or fish will be noticeably tastier and juicier.

Makes 1 gallon

½ gallon water
1 cup lightly packed brown sugar
1 cup kosher salt
Any or all of the following spices:
2 tablespoons black peppercorns, crushed
2 teaspoons bay leaves, finely ground
1 tablespoon coriander seeds, crushed
1 tablespoon juniper berries, crushed
1 quart ice cubes
Cold water as needed

1. Bring water, sugar, salt, and spices of choice to a boil in a large saucepan. Simmer 1 minute.
2. Pour into a measuring container that holds a gallon. Add ice cubes, then add cold water up to the 1-gallon mark. Stir until ice melts and brine is cool.

Brining times:

Trout fillets	15 minutes
Salmon steaks, up to 1 inch thick	30 minutes
Salmon steaks, more than 1 inch thick	45 minutes
Salmon, full side (fillet with skin)	Overnight
Pork loin and whole chickens	Overnight
Whole turkeys	Overnight
Whole turkeys, more than 15 pounds	Two nights

Notes:
+ The thicker the food, the more forgiving it is timewise.
+ When brining, just cover the food with brine. Don't use too much.
+ Use a timer for short brine times so you don't overdo it.

Balsamic vinegar reduction

Why reduce vinegar? Because it creates a thick sauce with a mouthwatering, concentrated flavor. It's nice to have on hand to drizzle on tomatoes, roasted or grilled vegetables, salads, roasted pork or chicken, tofu, even vanilla ice cream with strawberries (a classic Italian flavor combination).

Makes 1 cup

2 cups balsamic vinegar

1. Place vinegar in a small saucepan. Boil until the vinegar is reduced by half, to about 1 cup. Cool 10 minutes and place in a plastic squeeze bottle or a glass jar with a lid. Keep refrigerated for up to 1 month. Warm slightly before using (heat in 5-second increments in the microwave until pourable).

   Notes:
   + Moderately priced vinegar is fine for this recipe.
   + Do not use aged balsamic vinegar for this recipe. The flavor of fifteen- to-twenty-year-old balsamic is already concentrated.
   + High-quality balsamic vinegar takes years to make. Its rise in popularity has resulted in a lot of mediocre brands on the market. Look for "balsamico di Modena" on the label. As in the world of wine, generally speaking, you get what you pay for.

Braised garlic

I love the creamy texture and mellow flavor of these sautéed and simmered garlic cloves. Use whole braised-garlic cloves to garnish appetizers and pasta dishes, or serve a bowlful with an antipasto spread.

Makes 1½ cups

2 tablespoons canola oil
2 cups whole peeled garlic cloves*
1½ cups water
1 teaspoon kosher salt

1. Heat the oil in a small saucepan over high heat until almost smoking. Add garlic cloves and fry, stirring, until browned all over. Add water and salt, and bring to a boil.
2. Reduce heat and simmer, covered, for ½ hour. Cloves should be soft but still retain their shape.

Peeled garlic cloves, available at most supermarkets, are convenient for this recipe.

Notes:
+ The flavor of the garlic will depend on how long you cook the cloves in oil. Dark-brown cloves taste like roasted garlic. Light-brown cloves taste more like poached garlic.
+ Braised garlic is a great thickener; purée and add to dressings and sauces, such as **Braised garlic cream sauce**, page 186.

Caramelized onions

Onions are one of the great flavor bases in cookery; when caramelized, their flavor is "squared." Soft, sweet, and mellow, these slow-cooked onions are worlds away from the tear-inducing raw ingredient.

Makes about 5 cups

4 large yellow onions
¼ cup olive or canola oil
1 teaspoon kosher salt

1. Peel and slice onions into half moons: cut in half from top to bottom, then into ⅛-inch slices. They should look like crescent moons.
2. In the biggest-diameter pan you have, heat olive oil over high heat until it is almost smoking. Add onions and salt, lower heat to medium, and stir frequently with a wooden spoon until onions are soft and lightly browned, about 10 to 12 minutes. Reduce heat to low, cover pan, and cook another 15 minutes, stirring occasionally. Add salt. If you want browner or drier onions, cook uncovered 5 more minutes, scraping the bottom often.
3. Spread onions out on a baking pan and cool.

   Notes:
   + A large pan is important: more surface area creates more heat, which will caramelize the onions better. Use a heavy pan (not nonstick) for best results.
   + If you want more color/caramelization you can add some sugar (about 1 tablespoon) and cook the onions longer. This can be taken to extremes: the onions can be cooked until very brown and reduced to almost nothing, as for French onion soup.
   + Other possible additions are red wine vinegar and sugar; pomegranate molasses; red wine and sugar; and cranberry juice concentrate.
   + For a quick balsamic-onion relish: mix 1 cup caramelized onions with 4 tablespoons **Balsamic vinegar reduction.** Add salt to taste. Serve with roasted or grilled pork or chicken.
   + Use caramelized onions to top flatbread or pizzas; mix with focaccia dough for onionbread; or use with vegetarian dishes such as **Mushroom stroganoff** or **Stuffed portobello mushrooms**; or purée and use to thicken a sauce.

Chipotle barbecue sauce

Sweet, sour, hot, smoky, and a snap to make. Who needs to buy barbecue sauce from a store?

Makes 6 cups

¼ cup **Chipotle purée** (page 197)
½ cup cider vinegar
1 quart ketchup
¼ cup soy sauce
¼ cup molasses
¼ cup lightly packed light brown sugar
2 teaspoons granulated garlic
2 teaspoons granulated onion
2 teaspoons black pepper
1 teaspoon white pepper
½ cup orange juice

1. Make **Chipotle purée**.
2. Whisk all ingredients together well.

   Notes:
   + This sauce keeps for at least two weeks in the refrigerator. It will thicken as it sits; to thin, whisk in a little water.
   + This sauce can be habit-forming. Try serving it with pork or brushing it on salmon steaks before grilling.

Chipotle purée

This simple, smoky purée is much more convenient to use than whole chiles.

Makes about 1¼ cups

1 (7-ounce) can chipotle chiles in adobo sauce
Water

1. Place contents of can in a blender. Add water to the can until it is about ⅔ full. Swirl water around can to rinse well, then pour water into blender.
2. Blend on high speed 10 seconds, or until completely smooth.

Note:
+ Use leftover purée on quesadillas, in almost any kind of salsa, and for rubs and marinades. Refrigerate, or freeze extra purée in an ice cube tray; transfer frozen cubes to a zip-top plastic bag.

Custard sauce

Traditionally, custard sauce, or crème anglaise, is cooked twice—which is tricky because the egg yolks can curdle. I learned the simple technique used here from a pastry chef in Lyon, France.

Makes 2 cups

5 egg yolks
1½ cups whipping cream
½ cup plus 2 tablespoons sugar
Pinch of kosher salt
1 teaspoon vanilla extract

1. Place egg yolks in a small bowl and set aside.
2. Place cream, sugar, and salt in a small, heavy saucepan and bring to a boil, stirring occasionally to dissolve sugar.
3. Remove from heat and immediately whisk about half of the hot cream mixture into the egg yolks. Add this mixture back into the hot cream in the saucepan. Whisk to combine, cover the pan, and let sit for 10 minutes.
4. Pour custard through mesh strainer, stir in vanilla, cover bowl with plastic wrap, and chill.

Notes:
+ Egg whites can be frozen in a plastic zip-top bag for later use.
+ Custard sauce can be made with half-and-half instead of cream, but it will not be quite as thick.
+ The degree of risk associated with harmful bacteria in raw eggs can vary. Use only raw eggs purchased from a reliable source. For more information, see the American Egg Board website, www.aeb.org.
+ Custard sauce is extremely versatile. Serve plain or flavor with coffee crystals, brandy, Frangelico, or Grand Marnier.

Easy garlic croutons

Caesar salad is unthinkable without these crunchy morsels—and they're equally good in soups and other salads.

Makes 3 cups

½ pound bread (with crust), cut into ½-inch cubes (about 3 cups)
2 tablespoons good olive oil
¼ teaspoon kosher salt
⅛ teaspoon black pepper
1 teaspoon granulated garlic

1. Preheat oven to 325°.
2. Place bread cubes in a large mixing bowl. Drizzle cubes with oil, tossing cubes to distribute oil evenly. Add salt, pepper, and garlic and toss again. Spread cubes in a single layer on a baking pan.
3. Bake 8 minutes, then stir croutons to ensure even browning. Bake 8 to 10 minutes more, or until croutons are light brown and very dry.

Notes:
+ I like a good sourdough bread for croutons, crust and all, but almost any type of bread can be used.
+ Granulated garlic is slightly yellower and coarser than powdered, with the real flavor of garlic.

Pastry cream

This type of custard is a standard in the pastry chef's repertoire. It is used to fill éclairs, breakfast pastries, and cakes.

Makes 2½ cups

1 cup whole or low-fat milk
1 tablespoon plus 2 teaspoons cornstarch
¼ cup plus 2 tablespoons sugar
Pinch of kosher salt
1 egg
1 teaspoon vanilla extract

1. Bring milk just to a boil in a heavy saucepan (preferably stainless steel).
2. Whisk cornstarch, sugar, salt, egg, and vanilla together in a mixing bowl. Pour in hot milk, whisking constantly. Return mixture to the saucepan and cook over medium-high heat until custard bubbles, whisking constantly. Continue cooking as it boils for 3 to 5 seconds. The custard must boil briefly to thicken correctly and to cook out the raw cornstarch taste.
3. Place custard in a small bowl. Press plastic wrap onto the surface of the custard to prevent a skin from forming on top, and refrigerate 20 minutes, or until cold.

Notes:
+ When bringing milk to a boil, stir a few times—it's easy to burn the bottom.
+ If custard seems lumpy, whisk vigorously before using. If lumps persist, process a few seconds until smooth in food processor.

Quick pizza sauce

This sauce is thicker and more concentrated than marinara, so it will stick to a pizza crust and provide a strong flavor-base for cheese and other toppings.

Makes 2¾ cups

1 (6-ounce) can tomato paste
1 (15-ounce) can tomato sauce
2 teaspoons granulated garlic
2 teaspoons granulated onion
1 tablespoon Italian seasoning
1 tablespoon dried basil
1 teaspoon kosher salt
½ teaspoon black pepper
¼ teaspoon red chile flakes

1. Whisk all ingredients together.
2. Store for up to 6 days in refrigerator, or freeze in zip-top bags for up to 2 months.

Notes:
- If you have fresh basil, by all means omit the tablespoon of dried basil and add ¼ cup chopped fresh basil.
- For garlic lovers: spread this sauce on pizza dough or French bread, then sprinkle with minced fresh garlic before finishing with toppings.

Raspberry sauce

Ruby red, with a luscious mouthfeel—this is one of the easiest and most useful dessert sauces.

Makes ¾ cup

1 (12-ounce) bag frozen raspberries
3 tablespoons powdered sugar

1. Thaw berries completely, saving the juice that seeps out of them.
2. Place the berries, juice, and sugar in a food processor and run until smooth (about 4 seconds). Push mixture through a mesh strainer or food mill to remove seeds.

Roasted red peppers

Roasting fresh peppers intensifies their flavor. Puréed roasted peppers have a wonderful silky texture.

Makes about 1 cup

2 red bell peppers
1 teaspoon canola or salad oil

1. Preheat oven to 400°.
2. Coat peppers with oil, place on a baking pan, and bake 15 minutes. Turn peppers, then bake 15 more minutes, or until they have black patches all over. Plunge peppers immediately into cold water and chill for 10 minutes or so.
3. Peel peppers and remove seeds. Drain well.

Notes:
+ After peeling and seeding the peppers, store them in plastic zip-top bags for up to 5 days in the refrigerator. They're handy for salsas, spreads, salads, and pasta dishes, and make pretty garnishes when cut into thin strips.
+ Try dressing thin strips of red (or mixed color) roasted peppers with extra-virgin olive oil, a splash of balsamic vinegar, and salt and pepper. Use as a topping for grilled chicken breasts.
+ This method works well for all sorts of fresh peppers; but remember, if roasting spicy peppers, especially large amounts, use rubber gloves when peeling and seeding them.
+ Use a bowl of water to dip peppers in when peeling and seeding.
+ Peppers can also be roasted directly over a flame or on a grill: Just place peppers on a grill, or on a rack over a stove burner; roast until blackened and blistered, turning as needed.
+ Purée roasted peppers and use for dressings (see **Roasted red pepper–sherry dressing**); sauces (heat up the purée, whisk in some butter, add a dash of salt, a squeeze of lemon, and serve with a piece of grilled salmon or chicken); as a main ingredient in soups; or as a garnish for other soups.

Roasted tomatoes

Where can you find flavorful tomatoes year-round? How about your own refrigerator!

Makes about 2 cups

2 pounds (about 12) fresh Roma tomatoes
2 tablespoons canola, olive, or salad oil

1. Preheat oven to 300°.
2. Cut tomatoes in half lengthwise. Toss with oil to coat, and place on a parchment paper–lined baking pan, cut side down.
3. Roast 1 hour. Rotate pan front to back, then roast 30 minutes more. Skins will be cracked and blistered. Cool, peel, place in plastic tubs or zip-top bags, and store in refrigerator for up to 5 days.

   Notes:
   + These tomatoes can be cooked longer at a lower temperature, or even overnight, to really concentrate flavors, but this is the quick version.
   + Tomatoes can be tossed with salt and pepper or other spices such as chile flakes or fennel seed before roasting. I prefer not to add spices until later, since tomatoes are going to be peeled after baking, which strips off most of the flavor.
   + Pack in plastic zip-top bags and freeze for later use.
   + Try topping vegetarian dishes such as **Stuffed portobello mushrooms** with a tomato half; chopping for salsas or relishes; puréeing for soups or sauces; carefully scooping out seeds and filling halves with tuna salad, curried chicken salad, or smoked trout salad and serving atop dressed greens; marinating in good olive oil, minced fresh garlic, kosher salt, and black pepper, and using to decorate other foods, or chop first and then marinate to create an antipasto.

Spicy marinara sauce

This quick sauce is perfect for spontaneous spaghetti dinners.

Makes 1 quart

1 bay leaf
¼ teaspoon red chile flakes
½ teaspoon fennel seeds
¼ cup olive oil
½ cup minced onion
¼ cup minced celery
¼ cup minced carrot
2 tablespoons minced fresh garlic
½ cup dry white wine
1 (28-ounce) can tomato sauce
¼ cup water
1 tablespoon dried basil
½ teaspoon black pepper
2 teaspoons kosher salt

1. Grind bay leaf finely in an electric spice or coffee mill; add chile flakes and fennel seeds to grinder and PULSE a few times until they are broken up but not powdered.
2. In a medium saucepan over medium heat, heat olive oil until it shimmers. Add onion, celery, and carrot. Cook, stirring, for 2 minutes. Add garlic and stir 10 seconds. Add wine and boil 1 minute.
3. Add tomato sauce. Rinse tomato sauce can with the water and add liquid to saucepan. Add all spices and seasonings. Simmer, covered, 10 minutes.

Notes:

+ Toss this sauce with almost any kind of pasta; use it to make lasagna, manicotti, or cannelloni; serve with **Soft polenta with Asiago cheese** or **Stuffed portobello mushrooms**; or thin with stock and use with baked stuffed cabbage.
+ Try adding sliced, sautéed bell peppers; sausages, meatballs, bacon, or cooked ground beef or turkey; or frozen, dried, and crumbled extra-firm tofu.

Sweetened whipped cream

The traditional topping for pastries, desserts, and ice cream creations might just find a place on top of your morning coffee.

Makes 2½ cups/Enough for 8 to 10 desserts

1 cup whipping cream
2½ tablespoons powdered sugar
¼ teaspoon vanilla extract

1. Place all ingredients in a medium bowl. Using a whisk or hand-held electric mixer, whip to desired stage: soft-peak for folding into other ingredients, firm-peak for use on its own.

Sweet-sour syrup

Jesse McQuarrie, a wonderful chef I worked with, makes a sauce that inspired this versatile syrup.

Makes 1¾ cups

1 cup seasoned rice wine vinegar
¾ cup sugar
⅛ teaspoon red chile flakes (optional)
1 tablespoon lime juice

1. Bring the vinegar, sugar, and chile flakes to a boil in a small saucepan, preferably stainless steel. Remove from heat and stir in lime juice.
2. Syrup will keep, covered, in the refrigerator for a month.

   Note:
   + I keep this syrup around at all times, using it instead of a pinch of sugar in dressings or sauces. It is also a good topping for sushi rice, steamed spinach with toasted sesame seeds, and thinly sliced cucumbers.

Tamari-roasted pumpkinseeds

These baked seeds can be eaten as a snack, sprinkled on salads, blended in dressings and sauces, or used to garnish enchiladas, chiles rellenos, or mole.

Makes 2 cups

2 cups pumpkinseeds
1 tablespoon tamari sauce

1. Preheat oven to 350°. Toss seeds with tamari until fully coated.
2. Bake on a lightly oiled baking pan 5 minutes, then turn seeds on pan to cook evenly and bake 3 or 4 minutes more, until well browned. You may hear some seeds pop during baking. Cool slightly before using.

Teriyaki sauce

Teriyaki sauce

Teriyaki sauce is a wonderful marinade for chicken, fish, and tofu, as well as beef. Try some fried dishes or over steamed rice.

Makes 3½ cups

¼ cup chopped fresh ginger, tightly packed
7 cloves garlic
1 cup soy sauce
¾ cup frozen pineapple juice concentrate, thawed
1 tablespoon sambal oelek chili garlic sauce*
½ cup lightly packed light brown sugar
1½ cups water

1. Place all ingredients in a blender. Blend until smooth, about 10 seconds.

* Sambal oelek is available in Asian markets or the Asian foods section of some grocery stores. The brand I use comes in an 8-ounce jar with a rooster on the front. For more information, see Resources: Asian Ingredients.

Three chile purée

Use this rich purée in vegetable sautés, salsa, or enchilada or barbecue sauces.

Makes 3 quarts

½ pound dried pasilla chiles
½ pound dried ancho chiles
½ pound dried New Mexico chiles
1 gallon water
2 teaspoons kosher salt

1. Wearing rubber gloves, stem and seed all chiles. Bring chiles, water, and salt to a boil in a stockpot. Reduce heat and simmer, covered, 30 minutes.
2. In a blender, process chile mixture until smooth. Push mixture through a mesh strainer.

   Notes:
   + To avoid hot mixture spraying out of blender, do not fill container more than halfway and cover lid with a towel before turning on machine!
   + For straining, use a food mill or a ladle-strainer combination, using the ladle to push the mixture through the strainer.
   + I like the complexity of three kinds of chiles, but any one or two of the varieties above will work fine.
   + Mix with mayonnaise for a Southwestern-style crab dip or sandwich spread, or a topping for huevos rancheros.
   + Freeze extra purée in small containers or plastic zip-top bags.

Resources

Hints and Tips

This section contains advice for cooks. First I offer some general advice on cooking, then specific tips about work habits, baking, and more.

Correct cooking technique is crucial to success in the kitchen. There are many ways to cook any dish and endless ways to experiment with accompaniments, but there are also some basic rules in cookery that cannot be improved upon. For example, vegetables must never be overcooked. Meat or poultry for a stew should be well browned in the pan, and the caramelized bits thus produced must be incorporated into the stew. Cream and egg whites must never be overwhipped, desserts must be sweet but not overly so. There are many other rules that experience will teach.

Here are a few more guidelines that help shape my menus:

- Food should not be bland. This doesn't mean that everything should be drenched in a rich sauce or salted into oblivion. It means that seasoning is about enhancing and complementing an ingredient's natural flavor: red chard might be mixed with caramelized onions and a dash of balsamic vinegar; broccoli could have a sprinkling of sesame oil and rice wine vinegar; and meat, fish, and poultry should always have a flavorful marinade, accompanying sauce, or condiment like chutney, relish, or salsa.

- Food is more elegant and interesting when accompanied by a sauce. Sauces coat vegetables, accompany meat, fish, poultry, and tofu, and complement desserts.

- Dressings should always be made with high-quality oils and vinegars. They should be as full-flavored as possible.

- Desserts must be fresh, colorful, and a bit luxurious. I look for peak-of-season fruits and offer guests indulgences like chocolate and ice cream as well.

Be very careful when blending hot liquids: never fill a blender more than half full, cover with a towel before turning on, and PULSE on and off quickly before turning on continuously, to prevent hot liquid from spraying out the top.

Be careful with salt. You can always add more salt, but you can never subtract it. Salt should heighten flavor. Generally, if you can taste salt, you've used too much. With meat and poultry, however, it takes a bit of effort to oversalt.

It's much easier to thin a sauce than to thicken it. When making purées from frozen fruit, drain the juice from the defrosted fruit, then add only as much liquid as is needed to purée in the food processor or food mill; add juice at the end if needed.

Stay organized and clean up as you go. Everything in the kitchen goes more smoothly if you do.

Store everything you can in plastic, not glass, in the refrigerator. If glass breaks, it ruins whatever you're working on.

continued⟶

Fresh flavors are a lot different from cooked ones. Flavors can get "muddled" if cooked in a sauce or dressing. If you like a particular flavor a lot, consider adding it fresh at the end, even if you've used it at the beginning of a recipe. I like to do this with garlic and ginger, for example. Some things are best drizzled on just before serving: truffle oil on pasta or soups, lemon or lime juice on seafood, and liqueurs like Frangelico or Kahlua on desserts.

For sautéeing, canola oil works beautifully. It has a neutral flavor and a high smoke point. Olive oil also has a high smoke point, but its distinctive flavor isn't right for everything. The ethnicity of the dish determines the type of oil: Asian- and Mexican- inspired dishes start with peanut, canola, or salad oil, whereas anything Italian starts with olive (or sometimes butter).

If you like to cook with butter, mix equal parts of canola oil and drawn butter (melted butter with the watery portion that sinks and the salty foam that floats removed, leaving only pure yellow butterfat). This mixture retains the taste of butter while raising the smoke point so the butter won't burn at high temperatures.

To get that last bit out of a whipping cream carton, after you've turned it upside down and it seems empty, place it on its side for a few minutes, preferably in a warm spot. You'll be surprised how much more comes out.

When boiling cream, always use a larger pot than you think you need so the cream will have room to boil up and not over.

Use a narrow-bladed knife to cut sticky things like potatoes or cheese, or you'll spend a lot of time pulling the knife away from the food.

When roasting things in the oven (vegetables, chicken breasts, or potatoes), don't overcrowd them or pile them too deep (almonds, coconut, or sesame seeds), as they won't cook evenly.

Leave the fat layer on top of chicken stock when you refrigerate it. Fat seals out air and helps it keep longer (scrape it off with a spoon before heating). If frozen with the fat, melt it off under hot tap water before thawing the stock.

When making dressings with mayonnaise, lighten the calorie content by mixing half-and-half with sour cream. For the lowest fat, replace mayonnaise with nonfat yogurt.

Forget to add the last ingredient to a recipe sometimes? Put the ingredient on the counter where you know you're going to be finishing the recipe, either with a measuring spoon next to it or pre-measured in a measuring cup.

Always wash lettuce and leafy vegetables in a large bowl of cold water, then lift the greens out and place in a colander to drain. Dumping the bowl's contents into a colander results in the dirt going back on top of the lettuce.

When measuring honey, microwave it briefly—try 10 seconds at a time—to reliquefy it. This makes it much easier to pour and measure.

Always wipe off the underside of your stand mixer—the part where the whisk attaches—before clipping in the bowl. This will prevent residue falling into your bowl.

When a recipe says "don't overmix," turn off your mixing machine a little early and whisk or fold the last few turns by hand.

Never throw away flavor! For example, when cooking meat or poultry in a pan, always DEGLAZE the pan (add some liquid to the hot pan after removing meat and scrape the browned bits together, then use for the sauce to accompany meat). Rinse cans, especially when they contain thick liquids like tomato sauce, with a little water before recycling (use this liquid in the recipe you're working on). Water used to cook vegetables can be used for soup or pasta. When you can, use flavored liquids instead of water. For example, to deglaze a pan, one might use wine, fruit juice, or a flavored vinegar. For sauté dishes and stir fries I use dry white wine, sherry, orange juice, sake, or beer for deglazing.

Generally it is best to cool foods rapidly—especially meat, fish or poultry, or liquids made from them. Metal cools faster than plastic; large surface areas cool faster than small. A long metal spoon stuck into a container of hot liquid will help heat exchange. So, you might pour a hot stock into a wide metal pan, stick a long metal spoon into it, cover loosely, and refrigerate until cold. The liquid can then be portioned into plastic zip-top bags and frozen.

Work Habits: Safety and Efficiency

If you have a large kitchen, keep little ramekins of salt and pepper near all work stations; this saves some running around. Restaurant trick: premix salt and pepper (2:1) and keep near the stove. Garbage cans should also be conveniently located near busy areas.

Always put a moist towel or a piece of knobby plastic mat (found at hardware stores) under cutting boards to keep them from sliding around (very dangerous).

Boil leftover red wine until reduced by half and refrigerate or freeze for later use (try mixing it with a splash of balsamic vinegar and a dash of soy sauce, heat, and swirl in a little butter; this makes a delicious sauce for grilled meats).

Chop onions on a small cutting board (even if you have a nice butcher block or wooden counter) and carry the board to the stove. This prevents unpleasant odors from building up on your wooden counter, and is a safer method than walking across the kitchen with a hot pan.

Stir frying? Place the cut vegetables (or whatever you're going to cook) in a mixing bowl, with plastic wrap between layers, in the order they're going to be used. For example, onions go on top (to be fried first), then celery, then bell peppers, then zucchini on the bottom of the bowl, since it cooks very quickly.

Dress salads at the last minute—potato, pasta, and rice salads especially—or the flavor will fade. Taste starchy salads like these before serving; they may need perking up with salt and/or vinegar.

continued——➔

Hints and Tips continued

Pastry and Baking

When prebaking pie or sweet dough, you'll often have cracks when you remove the beans or rice that you used to weigh it down. Save a little dough when rolling out to patch small holes or cracks. If you forget to save any, patch holes with dabs of cream cheese before filling (especially with liquid fillings such as quiche batter or pecan pie filling).

Always drain vegetables well after sautéeing for a quiche, or the filling will be too juicy. Cooked or thawed spinach must be squeezed until almost dry.

There are many types of ovens, but some things don't change: It's usually hottest at the top. Don't crowd ingredients on a baking pan. Food cooks best when it has room around it. This goes both for items on a baking pan and for racks holding the pans. If the racks are very close together, air circulation is reduced and food may not cook evenly and may take longer to cook.

Cheese

After opening and cutting jack or other mild cheeses, sprinkle lightly with kosher salt before rewrapping; they will keep a lot longer.

Use leftover pieces of white cheese to make a cheese-milk sauce (Mornay); blue cheese bits make a nice sauce for pasta, or mix with soft butter and serve over grilled steak.

Freeze any cheese you won't use in a week except hard, salted cheeses such as Parmesan. Use later for sauces or soups. (See also **Blue cheese "snow."**)

Eggs

Look for a thin-edged bowl to crack your eggs on or you'll end up with little pieces of shell in your recipe. Always crack your eggs into a bowl before pouring them into your batter. This way you can see any shell bits that fall to the bottom. It is much easier and faster than picking shells out of the batter.

Most pastry recipes work best with eggs at room temperature or even warm. I take my eggs out of the fridge when I'm starting a recipe and run hot tap water over them for 5 to 10 minutes. (You may see bubbles rise from the egg's shell; don't worry. As the egg warms up, some air escapes through the porous shell.)

When making something that calls for egg yolks (custard sauce or pastry cream) separate your eggs into measuring cups. Save the whites and freeze in zip-top bags. Label with date and amount (in cups, and number of whites). When thawing, put plastic bag in a bowl and set in a warm place or, if rushed, put bag inside another zip-top bag and set in a big bowl of hot water. Make sure water doesn't go over the opening of the bag, as few bags are truly watertight.

Herbs

Herbs fall into two categories, delicate (cilantro, parsley, basil) and robust (sage, bay, thyme). The robust herbs are best for drying and long cooking. Delicate herbs are best used fresh, at or near the end of cooking.

Cilantro is the most delicate. Heat destroys its flavor, and even fine chopping diminishes it. Chop it coarsely and keep it cool. Basil cooks well (think pizza Margherita), but, like many herbs, it turns black quickly after being chopped. To avoid this, cover herbs with olive oil or water immediately after chopping. Most herbs will last a day or two like this, if refrigerated. COMPOUND BUTTERS are a great way of preserving the flavors of fresh herbs. Store in the freezer for up to two months.

Many sources claim that dried herbs are more concentrated than fresh and one should use half as much. I've never found this to be true. Furthermore, the flavor of many store-bought dried herbs is at best dusty, at worst unrecognizable.

There are three types of herbs:

1. Store-bought dried: consistent, good for cooked dishes, but who knows how old?

2. Homemade dried: similar in flavor to fresh, mostly because they're usually not very old. Nice to have on hand and easy to make: just gather herbs, tie together at the stems, and hang upside down in a dry place for a week or so. When they get dry and crumbly, strip them from the stems and put them in small jars.

3. Fresh: always best. I love the flavor of fresh herbs in dressings, marinades, COMPOUND BUTTERS, soups—just about everything.

The best way to wash herbs is in a bowl of water, before stemming or chopping. Leave tie on stems and dip the herbs in a bowl of water a few times. Then "throw" water out, swinging the herb forcefully (this should be done outside). Blot herbs on paper or cloth towels before chopping; the drier the herb, the longer it will hold for other uses. Most herbs must be picked off the stems before using, except cilantro. The delicate stems are easily incorporated when chopped with the leaves.

Store fresh herbs in the refrigerator wrapped in a moist towel inside a plastic bag. For large quantities, place herbs in a plastic container with the cut stems in water and a plastic bag draped over them. They will last two or three times as long this way.

In the Sonoma area, rosemary is so prolific, it's practically a civic duty to cook with it. Bay trees are abundant in the woods, and many other herbs grow almost like weeds: oregano, mint, even lemongrass. Fruit trees often produce more than the owner can use: Meyer lemon, persimmon, and fig, for example. Look around, ask questions, befriend neighbors—you might be surprised at what's growing near you.

continued ⟶

Tofu and Soy Products

Tofu is one of the best sources of protein for a vegetarian diet. One East Asian proverb refers to it as "meat without a bone." Tofu is high in vitamins and minerals, and low in calories and saturated fats. Made from soybeans, tofu becomes a complimentary protein when combined with grains such as rice. On top of all this, tofu is inexpensive and versatile. Its neutral flavor lends itself to countless methods of preparation.

Some of the commonly available soybean products are:

- **Silken tofu:** Use for desserts (lightly steamed, with maple syrup or honey), in dressings as a thickener (emulsifier), and for spreads in place of mayonnaise.

- **Firm or extra-firm tofu:** Use scrambled, in stir-frys, burritos, tostadas, and chili; cubed for brochettes, soups, and curries; cut into slices ("cutlets"), breaded and fried, or marinated and then grilled, baked, or smoked.

- **Miso, white or red:** Use in soups, dressings, marinades, sauces to accompany tofu, and vegetables (see Green beans with easy miso sauce).

- **Tempeh:** A fermented soybean cake with a firm, chunky texture, tempeh can be used in much the same way as extra-firm tofu.

- **Soy milk:** Use in almost any recipe that calls for milk. The final product will not be as rich as when made with milk.

There are also many processed tofu products available in markets, often designed to imitate a meat or dairy product: tofu mozzarella, tofu pepperoni, and tofu hot dogs, to name a few.

Some techniques for using tofu:

- Try freezing firm or extra-firm tofu, thawing, squeezing dry, and mashing. Use for chili, in burritos, or casseroles. The freezing-thawing process transforms the texture into a ground beef–like texture.

- I prefer extra-firm tofu because it is sturdy and versatile. Drain it, squeeze out as much moisture as possible, then cut into slabs, or "cutlets." Press each slab with paper towels until very little moisture comes out, then lay out on more paper towels sprinkled lightly with kosher salt, then sprinkle the tofu again with kosher salt, add another layer of paper towels, and let sit 5 to 10 minutes. For a really dry tofu, put a baking pan on top and weight the tofu for another 10 minutes. This process dries, firms, and seasons the tofu, and works for most of the ways I like to prepare it.

- For some recipes I cut tofu into cubes, salt it, spread it out on an oiled baking pan, then bake it for about 20 minutes at 300°. This dries it out and produces a "skin," which makes the tofu sturdier when combined with a sauce.

- Edamame, or soybeans in the pod, are an easy, healthful snack food with a rich, nutty flavor. Look for them in the freezer section of the market, and boil (right from the freezer) 4 to 6 minutes. Toss lightly with kosher salt after cooking, then cool.

- Flavor it, season it, "texture" it, sauce it (see **Corn chip–crusted tofu with fresh tomato salsa**).

For (much) more on tofu, see Shurtleff and Aoyagi's wonderful resource, *The Book of Tofu*, 1983, Ten Speed Press.

Vegetables

In cooking school I learned to BLANCH vegetables in boiling, salted water, and SHOCK them in ice water to stop the cooking. This is a very useful technique. I still blanch them the same way. A steamer is even better, as it doesn't "rinse" off as much flavor or vitamins. Often, though, I try to undercook them slightly, pull them out of the boiling water, then spread them out and cool on a baking sheet. This retains more flavor and nutrients than "bathing" the vegetables twice. However, if they're on the edge of being overdone, plunging the vegetables into an ice bath is the quickest way to stop cooking.

Roasting vegetables is a quick, clean method that concentrates flavors. Although most vegetables can be lightly coated with olive oil, sprinkled with salt and pepper, and roasted in a hot (375°–400°) oven until they're slightly soft, some of the harder vegetables require precooking. I like to blanch carrots, chayote, cauliflower, and rutabagas in boiling water briefly before roasting. Butternut squash roasts beautifully, with the addition of a little water to the baking pan so it stays moist. When roasting onions I often cover them with an upside-down baking pan so they do not burn.

Always sprinkle cut eggplant with kosher salt and let it rest for 10 minutes before cooking. Salting gets rid of excess moisture and seals the outer cell walls, which means the eggplant soaks up less oil when cooked. To roast, toss eggplant lightly with oil of choice, season, and lay out on oiled or parchment paper–lined baking sheets.

Meat, Fish, and Poultry

Always keep meat, fish, and poultry on the bottom of the fridge in case they drip.

Leave some fat on meat for roasting or grilling. Fat helps meat stay moist.

Meat and poultry taste better when roasted on the bone. Shrimp tastes better when cooked in its shell.

Roast meat for a meal earlier rather than later. It should rest at least 15 minutes before cutting, or a lot of moisture will be lost when it is cut.

Buy a smoked chicken at the market. Pull the meat off of the bones and make something wonderful—a pasta dish, cold salad, casserole, or soup. Make stock with the bones, then freeze it in small plastic zip-top bags. When you want a nice, smoky flavor in a dish (such as a sauce for steak, pasta, or soup), pull out a bag of smoky frozen stock.

Tools and Equipment

Having the right gear and keeping things clean and organized are two of the most important principles I use to manage the kitchen effectively and cook three meals a day. You can do the same in your kitchen.

This section describes some of my favorite tools. I find them extremely useful at Westerbeke Ranch, and most of them are equally valuable at home. Look for these items at restaurant supply stores, kitchen stores, and supermarkets. Also, ethnic markets and hardware stores are full of finds: inexpensive peelers, cleavers, and much more.

Bench knife/dough scraper This is a primarily a baker's tool, but I have found other applications for this unique utensil. A bench knife can be used for cutting gratins and casseroles right in their baking pans. Of course, it's for portioning dough and scraping excess flour off large work surfaces. If you like to bake and have a large cutting board, you'll appreciate a bench knife.

Chocolate chopper This utensil is sold as a chocolate chopper, but I call it the "ultimate icepick." Working with chocolate means chopping blocks down to small sizes to facilitate melting. The chocolate chopper, along with a stiff, sharp serrated knife, is simply the best tool for this chore. Look for choppers with at least three sharp-tipped tines.

Digital scale Although the ingredients in most recipes are measured in volume—cups, tablespoons, etc.—the most precise measurement is by weight. Pastry and baking recipes often list ingredients this way. Why? Pastry recipes must be more precise than savory recipes, and some common baking and sweet ingredients are difficult to measure exactly by volume. Examples include chocolate and flour. One of the best features of a digital scale is the "zero out" function, which makes precise measurement of multiple ingredients fast and easy. Take a chocolate truffle recipe calling for 8 ounces of chocolate and 2 ounces of butter as an example. With the scale turned on, put a measuring cup (preferably lightweight plastic) on the scale and hit "zero out," add chopped chocolate until it reads 8 ounces, hit "zero out" again, then add butter until it reads 2 ounces.

Electric spice or coffee grinder Spices and seeds are always best when freshly ground, and a small electric coffee grinder is the best tool for this operation. Usually priced around $15, coffee grinders can sometimes be found on sale in large department stores for $10. If you cook with spices a lot, consider buying a dedicated grinder for your spices, or your morning coffee may end up tasting like fennel seeds or cumin.

Ice cream scoops These are surprisingly useful when dealing with large quantities of food. Besides scooping ice cream, they can portion cookie dough, muffin batter, mashed potatoes, yams, and much more.

Instant-read thermometer Widely available, this little tool is extremely useful for cooking meat and poultry, especially roasts and turkeys.

Japanese mandolin A fantastic tool if you feed large numbers of people. There is nothing like it for making uniform slices of cucumber or carrot. It comes with replaceable blades for different cutting needs, such as shoestring or fettucine shapes. Essential for making spring roll filling and vegetable "ribbons." Available in Asian hardware stores or online (see Resources: Websites and Ordering Information).

Kitchen shears A good pair of kitchen shears is a crucial piece of equipment. Use for cutting small poultry such as quail and game hens, trimming flowers, even cutting pizza.

Knife sharpener This is a nice gadget to quickly restore a knife's edge. It won't work indefinitely; sometimes a knife needs to be ground on a sharpening stone or taken to a professional.

Knives It doesn't pay to skimp on cutlery. Chef's knives and paring knives are the essential ones. Brand preference is a personal choice. I prefer German and Japanese knives: Henckels, Mac, and Goldfish are some of my favorites. Inexpensive professional quality workhorse brands include Chicago Cutlery, Dexter-Russel, and Victorinox. Different companies make certain knives better than others. For example, Henckels makes one of the best chef's knives on the market, Victorinox makes my favorite (cheap!) paring knife, and the thin blades from Japan are fantastic tomato knives and vegetable cleavers. The things I look for are a thin blade, good balance, a comfortable grip, and a pleasing aesthetic. A good knife is a cook's best friend.

Ladles All ladles are not created equal. First there are the sizes: small and medium, for small amounts of sauces and plate presentation, as well as for pushing sauces and purées through strainers and china caps (china caps are restaurant-size food mills). Large ladles are useful for serving soup but also for pushing sauces through mesh strainers. Second, there is the manner in which they are constructed. Most are inexpensive and short-lived; the handle and the cup eventually come apart. Look for higher-quality one-piece ladles.

Lexan® measuring cups These utensils are a good example of the high-quality tools available in restaurant supply stores but not found in most home kitchens. Well, they should be! Lexan® measuring cups (and other containers) have all the benefits of glass, plus they are practically indestructible and comparatively inexpensive.

continued⟶

Tools and Equipment continued

Lime squeezer Called an *esprimador* in Spanish, this is one of my favorite tools. There's nothing like it for quickly juicing a few limes for salsa or for making Margaritas. Mexican markets usually carry the inexpensive models, or you can buy deluxe ones at kitchen supply stores.

Melon baller A specialized tool for making perfectly round melon balls. Can also be used for quickly coring halved apples and pears.

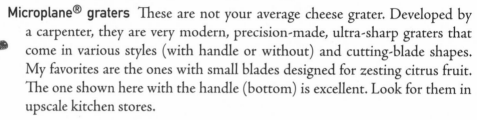

Microplane® graters These are not your average cheese grater. Developed by a carpenter, they are very modern, precision-made, ultra-sharp graters that come in various styles (with handle or without) and cutting-blade shapes. My favorites are the ones with small blades designed for zesting citrus fruit. The one shown here with the handle (bottom) is excellent. Look for them in upscale kitchen stores.

Japanese bonepullers and Needlenose pliers The Japanese have created an incredible array of specialized fish-handling tools. Most useful when working with large quantities of fish. For pulling the pinbones out of salmon fillets, nothing works like a bonepuller pictured here. Look for one in a Japanese hardware store or online.

Offset spatula This specialized tool smoothes out the icing on cakes. However, it also works better than a regular spatula for such things as smoothing out batters inside a cake pan, or spreading melted chocolate to an even thickness. Certainly not a necessity but an extremely useful tool for bakers, pastry chefs, and kitchen gadget nuts.

Pastry bag Also called a piping bag, this is an essential item for cake decorating, but it can also be used for filling pastries, placing chocolate mousse into cups without making a mess, and even piping savory mixtures such as meat stuffings. Pictured with various sizes of star and plain tips.

Permanent marking pens, self-stick labels, and masking tape Marking pens can be used to write descriptions of contents right on plastic zip-top bags. I often do this with items going into the refrigerator. Foods going into the freezer require a more durable solution. Masking tape works, but self-stick address labels are tidier and adhere just as well. Label anything that's going into the freezer with the name and date it was made, and when possible a use-by date as well. If a food item isn't too juicy, put the label just inside the top of the bag so that you can read it through the bag. This will ensure the sticker stays put. Always put the sticker in the same area of a bag so you know where to look for information when you need it. I like the upper left corner, which is easy to see when bags are arranged like books on a shelf.

Ramekins A number of the recipes in *Celebrating the Seasons* call for ramekins. Other uses: fill with soft butter and place directly on the dining table for parties, use for storing small amounts of freshly ground spices (or leftover sauces and dressings), fill with kosher salt and keep near the stove for convenient seasoning, or use for any number of hot and cold dessert preparations and any type of cobbler or crisp.

Sharpening steel A good sharpening steel is crucial for knife maintenance. I like the diamond-coated steels, which are somewhat oval in shape. They bring a knife back to sharpness quickly and last a long time. Also pictured—with the black handles—is the classic metal sharpening steel, used by butchers and fish cutters for centuries. Remember that a steel is for maintaining an edge, not sharpening a very dull knife. When a knife is really dull, it must be sharpened on a sharpening stone or taken to a professional sharpener. Knife shops are best, but sometimes hardware stores will sharpen knives.

Spray bottles Many hardware stores sell small plastic spray bottles. I like the nifty designer colors for home use. For sanitation: Fill a bottle most of the way with water and top with a capful of bleach (the California health department recommends one tablespoon bleach to one gallon water). Make sure to label this bottle. Use on cutting boards, sinks, sponges, the refrigerator, anything in the bathroom, even windows. For cooking: Fill a different-colored bottle with canola oil to spray your baking pans before dusting with flour or lining with parchment paper for a true nonstick surface. Or fill with olive oil to spray croutons before baking, items about to go on the grill, or vegetables about to be roasted. This technique is great if you cook often; if not, the oil may gum up the nozzle.

Spreaders I love searching for these at thrift stores and flea markets. Often available for pennies, they are the perfect tool for spreading mayonnaise on a sandwich, butter on toast, or cream cheese on a bagel, or for getting peanut butter out of the jar and correctly arranged on that stick of celery.

Squeeze bottles These are popular in restaurants for making pretty little dots of sauce on plates. They can be very useful at home for vinaigrettes and cold sauces such as chocolate, custard, caramel, and raspberry (hot sauces can get messy). For easy transport (to picnics, potlucks, or a friend's house) put vinaigrette or sauce ingredients in a squeeze bottle and a piece of plastic wrap over the neck *before* screwing on the top. When you arrive, remove and discard wrap, replace top, and use as needed.

continued——➔

Tools and Equipment

Surgical gloves These can be useful at home for peeling large amounts of chile peppers, handling things with slimy textures such as okra and chayote, or cleaning up.

Timers When you cook a lot, the odds are that you'll burn things now and again. Timers are a great help. It's nice to have two, because the more things you're working on, the more timers you need. They can be used as reminders: "There's the alarm. It's time to get the ice cream out of the freezer, so it will be the perfect texture when I need it."

Tongs How useful are tongs in the kitchen? Let me count the ways. Tongs are an essential piece of equipment. Of the many versions available, pictured here are the standard version and a sturdy, locking pair with rubber grips.

Towels One of the most important things in the kitchen. Most professional cooks use terrycloth, or bar, towels for everything in the kitchen—holding hot pans, cleaning up spills, cleaning off a knife between cake cuts, and a thousand other things. You can find these at supermarkets and auto supply stores. Note the two kinds of towels pictured here: terrycloth and tea towels are best for cleaning glassware.

Vegetable peelers Note the red plastic peeler, shown next to the classic metal one. Known as a Swiss peeler, it performs beautifully. Once you get used to the handle shape, it may become a favorite. It even peels thick-skinned vegetables such as butternut squash.

Whisks Thin tines are best all around; use for whipping cream, whisking butter or a cornstarch SLURRY into sauces, making pastry cream, etc. Thick-tined whisks are good for polenta and thick mixtures such as a chocolate and cream ganache.

Zester, channel knife This classic tool is useful for making thin strings of citrus zest, which can be used for garnish or diced and added to dressings and marinades. Creates a different shape of zest than the microplane grater. Note that one has a channel knife as well, which is useful for cutting decorative grooves along the length of cucumbers or carrots, which can then be sliced on rounds to create a fluted or floral shape.

Not pictured:

Cherry pitter A specialized tool but very useful for pitting cherries and olives. If you love cherries and want to extend their season by canning a few jars, or if you find yourself puzzling over how to get the pits out of a few dozen olives, then this is the tool you need.

226   Resources: Tools and Equipment

Cutting boards A very important piece of equipment. Plain white plastic boards can be found at restaurant supply and department stores. The important thing is that they're slightly textured—not totally smooth, which makes them slippery. Wood is great for larger boards and butcher block tables. Having a large piece of hardwood to work on makes cooking all the more pleasurable.

Freezer Freezers are a great labor-saver, but they're not right for everything. Some things simply freeze and thaw better than others (for example, shrimp and beef freeze well, salmon and lettuce do not). I pack leftovers in plastic zip-top bags, label them with self-stick address labels and/or a permanent marker (remember to put what it is, the date, and the quantity, if appropriate), and pat them flat in the freezer. When they're frozen I rearrange them standing up like books. (This saves a lot of space.) At any given time my "library of flavors" might contain clam chowder, chile verde, mole sauce, dried chile purée, roasted poblano purée, cooked beans, hummus, mushroom gravy, puréed chipotle chiles, cookie dough, compound butter (rolled in cylinders), and overripe bananas or other fruit.

Garlic press Very handy, and it saves cutting board clean-up. Look for well made (often Swiss or German) presses with that are easy to clean.

Mesh strainer I often refer to this tool as a wooden-handled strainer, to differentiate it from others in the kitchen. Very useful for removing seeds from purées and cooked bits from custards, for draining noodles, and much more.

Pans Restaurant supply stores have the best deals on good cookware, although sales at big department stores can sometimes compete (I've found great deals on coffee grinders, cutlery, and appliances). Best brands include Calphalon®, KitchenAid®, and All-Clad®. Expect to pay a lot and you won't be shocked. I like nonstick pans for eggs and crêpes, but that's about it. They just don't stand up to constant use. Still, for the home, a small (8-inch) nonstick pan is a great thing to have (I have two so I can cook two crêpes at once). Store them with a towel between each pan and they will last longer. If you have only one, wrap it in plastic wrap for storage.

Parchment paper Very useful if you cook a lot, especially for pastry work. Use parchment to line baking pans for cakes, egg strata, and all sorts of roasted foods, such as meat, poultry, vegetables, and candied nuts.

Zip-top plastic bags Great for storing almost anything. Always squeeze out all the air when closing and label with description, date, and quantity if appropriate. When freezing liquids (such as stock or leftover coconut milk) in bags, lay flat and fold closure up (prop against side of freezer so it stays). This will ensure no liquid escapes.

Asian Ingredients

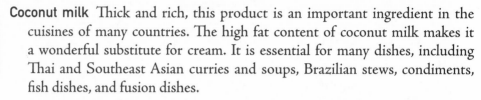

Shopping in ethnic markets is a wonderful way to find inspiration. Here are some of my favorite discoveries. Look for them in Asian markets or supermarkets, or online (see websites section).

Coconut milk Thick and rich, this product is an important ingredient in the cuisines of many countries. The high fat content of coconut milk makes it a wonderful substitute for cream. It is essential for many dishes, including Thai and Southeast Asian curries and soups, Brazilian stews, condiments, fish dishes, and fusion dishes.

Fish sauce (nam pla) This condiment is the Asian counterpart to anchovy paste. It adds depth of flavor to soups, dressings, and sauces. Use sparingly, as it is very strong.

Glass noodles are known by many names—saifun, harusame, bean thread, and cellophane noodles. Made from mung beans, they are white before cooking but turn clear after a few minutes in boiling water. When deep-fried they puff up dramatically, making a wonderful garnish for soups and salads. Use as for rice noodles; especially good in **Vietnamese spring rolls**. Pictured are a 10.5-ounce pack of 8 "nests," and a 5.29-ounce pack of 3 nests.

Rice noodles Made from either rice or mung beans, these noodles come in three widths: thin, medium, and wide. I find that the medium are the most versatile. They cook quickly and can be used in many dishes, including noodle bowls, soups and cold noodles with sauces (such as peanut), or in spring roll filling.

Sambal oelek chili garlic sauce Fans of spicy foods will love this sauce. Very spicy and pungent, it has a unique combination of garlic, chile, and vinegar flavors. Many of the recipes in this book rely on sambal oelek for its deep, earthy heat. Present it on the side when serving almost any type of Asian food.

Soy sauce Used as an ingredient and a condiment in many cuisines, soy sauce adds a complex, salty flavor. There are many types of soy sauce, such as shoyu (the Japanese word for soy sauce, made from half soy and half wheat), mushroom-flavored, and sweet. My favorite is tamari, which is a strong, aged soy sauce. Beware of very inexpensive soy sauces, as they are made in huge factories, and taste like it. Soy sauce has many applications and has found its way into dishes from various countries. Some brands are wheat-free.

Spring roll wrappers (bánh tráng) Opaque and very delicate when soaked in warm water, these wrappers can enclose a multitude of fillings. Serve raw or deep-fry.

Suki sauce This sauce is a delicious, spicy, sesame-flavored sauce. Use it on cold noodle dishes, in stir-frys, or with chicken or tofu dishes.

Sweet chili sauce This sweet and spicy sauce can be found in many home refrigerators. Try it on tofu, with fish or pork, or as a marinade for chicken. Thin with seasoned rice wine vinegar for a dipping sauce for eggrolls and dim sum.

Tamarind concentrate This ultra-sour flavor base is one of my favorite ingredients to experiment with. It can be found in many cuisines including Indian, Southeast Asian, and Latin American. In Mexico it is used in drinks, popsicles, and candies. When contrasted with a sweet flavor, it is wonderful in dipping sauces, relishes, and chutneys, as well as in marinades for pork and chicken. Look for a brand that is pure tamarind, with no additives.

Thai curry paste This is perhaps the single most useful prepared flavor paste to be found. Absolutely packed with flavor, three types of curry pastes are commonly available: red, green, and yellow. Only the yellow is vegetarian; the others contain shrimp paste. The wonderful blend of chiles, garlic, ginger, lemongrass, and other ingredients is used in many Thai restaurants for soups, dipping sauces, and, of course, curries. Buy some and find out how easy it is to make these dishes at home. For soup, start with chicken or vegetable broth and some coconut milk, then add vegetables of choice and cook halfway, add curry paste to taste, then add noodles and chicken or seafood; cook through, and serve with a squeeze of lime. For curries, simply use less stock, more vegetables, meat, fish, or chicken, and omit noodles. Serve with lime wedges and white rice.

Tom yum paste This sour soup base is rich with lemongrass flavor. Dissolve it in stock and incorporate your choice of noodles, vegetables, seafood, poultry, pork, beef, or tofu. Note: this is the only ingredient I recommend that contains monosodium glutamate.

Yields and Equivalents

This section is useful when you have measurement questions. For example, when a recipe calls for ½ cup chopped cilantro, do you need one or two bunches? If a recipe calls for ¼ cup chopped garlic, how many cloves do you need? Yields may vary slightly.

Fresh herbs: All measurements are for herbs that have been washed, dried, stemmed, and chopped, with the exception of cilantro. Cilantro stems are tender and do not need to be removed.

1 tablespoon	**equals approximately ¼ ounce**
1 bunch	**equals approximately:**
Basil	1 cup chopped
Cilantro	¾ cup chopped
Dill	1 cup plus 2 tablespoons chopped
Italian parsley	1¼ cup chopped
Mint	¾ cup chopped
Oregano	¾ cup chopped
Rosemary	5½ tablespoons chopped
Sage	½ cup chopped
Tarragon	7 tablespoons chopped
Thyme	6½ tablespoons chopped

Other ingredients:

Carrot	1 medium yields ½ cup plus 2 tablespoons finely diced
Celery	1 stalk yields ⅓ cup finely diced
Garlic	1 teaspoon minced=1 large clove; ¼ cup minced=10 large cloves
Ginger	Yields about 70 percent original weight when peeled. For example, 3 ounces whole ginger will yield about 2 ounces peeled, 6 ounces will yield about 4 ounces peeled, etc.
Green onion	1 bunch green onions yields 1 to 1¼ cups finely chopped
Lemon or Lime	About 2 tablespoons juice and about 2 teaspoons zest
Onion	1 medium yellow onion yields 1½ cups finely diced
Salad greens	1 pound spring mix (Mesclun or mixed greens) feeds 10 people generously, ¾ pound feeds 8 people, ½ pound feeds 6 people
Tofu	1 (14-ounce) block firm or extra-firm tofu yields 8 slices when cut like a loaf of bread, or 60 ½-inch cubes

If you want to scale a recipe up or down, you will need to know how many teaspoons are in a tablespoon or how many ounces are in a cup.

Liquid measure:

3 teaspoons	=	1 tablespoon
2 tablespoons	=	1 ounce
8 ounces	=	1 cup
2 cups	=	16 ounces or 1 pint
4 cups	=	32 ounces or 1 quart
4 quarts	=	128 ounces or 1 gallon

Ingredients can be measured by weight or by volume. Volume is related to capacity.

For liquid ingredients, volume and weight are interchangeable. If a recipe calls for 4 ounces of orange juice, you could use either a measuring cup or a scale.

Non-liquid ingredients are measured either by volume or by weight, but not both. For example, a recipe might call for 6 ounces of cocoa "by volume," which means you should measure the ingredient in a cup, not on a scale.

If you're cooking with someone who asks, "Can you measure 6 ounces of cocoa for me?" your reply should be, "By weight or volume?"

Websites and Ordering Information

The Internet is evolving so rapidly that some of the websites listed here may have changed by the time you search for them. The list below is a small sample of what is currently available in cyberspace.

Educational Resources

www.aeb.org American Egg Board site: learn about safe handling procedures and much more.

http://www.earthday.net Hundreds of educational links and ways to get involved in environmental causes.

http://www.earthsite.org The official Earth Day site, with links to learn more about the holiday, its founder, and ways to get involved.

http://www.foodsiteoftheday.com Here's the place to start almost any food-related search. The archive of more than 900 sites is mind-boggling, but, oddly, not in alphabetical order. There are links to "Firegirl" on chiles, Japanese Food Markets, The Catfish Institute, Foodie Central, the "Garlic Goddess," and The Screen Cuisine List at yumfood.com (125 movies about food). If you've got the time, this site has the links.

www.localharvest.org Great California site to find organic farms, restaurants, and organic produce home delivery programs.

http://www.mbayaq.org Monterey Bay Aquarium's attractive site. Go to "seafood watch" section to look up fish and check status: Overfished? Mercury issues? Huge bycatch? Very educational.

www.pastryscoop.com If you're curious about pastry, this site is worth a look: there are chocolate makers' percentage charts, a metric conversion calculator, and articles on famous restaurants and pastry chefs.

http://seafood.audubon.org More seafood information; downloadable seafood wallet card, coded from green to red. Informative, nicely designed.

http://www.slowfood.com Slow down and take a look at this site, which aims to "protect the pleasures of the table from the homogenization of fast food and modern life, through a variety of initiatives; it promotes gastronomic culture, develops taste education, conserves agricultural biodiversity, and protects traditional foods at risk of extinction." Full of interesting information, it also has menus and wine recommendations. Look for a group, or "convivia," near you.

www.thefutureoffood.com This site advertises the documentary of the same name, concerning genetic engineering and industrial agriculture in the U.S. and Canada. Links to learn more and get involved.

Food Writing and Information Sites

www.egullet.org Subtitled "the eGullet society for culinary arts and letters," this is one of the most intelligent culinary sites I've seen. It is organized around a forum section where conversations concerning all things food are ongoing, with regular "Q and A" sessions featuring some of the best chefs and authors in the world. The site links to the daily gullet archives, which is a list of irreverent, smart articles on a wide range of topics. "Grazing" this site is free, but to interact in the forums requires registration. Although the site is reorganizing as we go to press, it's worth checking in on.

www.sfgate.com/eguide/food A good resource about northern California. Articles, restaurant recommendations, news; no registration required.

Ingredients and Equipment

www.amazon.com The megastore of the Internet, which either sells or links you to what you seek.

www.asiafoods.com A limited store with a nice Asian food glossary, cooking technique section, and sushi primer with directions on how to roll sushi.

www.ethnicgrocer.com This online store has many ethnic ingredients and equipment.

www.kitchenconservatory.com Japanese mandolins, stainless steel cookware, recipes, and a stump-the-chef column.

Recipe Sites

www.gadnet.com/recipes.htm Indian recipes galore.

www.recipelink.com Heavy on the advertising, this site has a number of interesting sections and features: the cooking club forum will help you track down unusual recipes, the TV show links will direct you to recipes you may have seen, and the copycat recipes section prints recipes from restaurants.

www.recipes.chef2chef.net A very busy, ad-filled site with ask-a-chef feature, forums, top 100 recipes, and "the culinary guru," with conversion calculator and much more.

http://www.recipesource.com Formerly known as the Searchable Online Archive of Recipes, or SOAR, this is perhaps the biggest online recipe database and the place I always start a recipe search.

Chef John Littlewood and Westerbeke Ranch

www.hppress.com John Littlewood's website where you can order more books, visit John's photo gallery, learn about John's upcoming events, or just drop a line.

www.westranch.com For more information about Westerbeke Ranch, including a virtual tour, directions and booking information.

Glossary

BLANCH; BLANCHING. To briefly cook in boiling water. Often used with vegetables to partially cook them. Sometimes used to refer to quick cooking in hot oil.

COMPOUND BUTTER. A mix of soft butter and other ingredients. Also known as flavored butter. Compound butters have numerous variations, including classics like maitre-d'hôtel (parsley, black pepper, salt, and lemon juice), truffle, and anchovy. Making compound butters is a handy way to preserve flavor, since the butterfat holds the incorporated ingredients in stasis. For example, fresh herbs can be chopped, mixed with other flavorings and soft butter, rolled in plastic wrap, labeled, and frozen. The resulting compound butter can be used to top grilled meats, spread on toasted bread, or thicken and flavor sauces by whisking in at the end.

DEGLAZE. To add liquid (wine, stock, water, brandy, or any flavored liquid such as vegetable blanching water) to a pan to dissolve cooked or caramelized pieces. Useful for making pan sauces, especially when cooking meat, poultry, or fish.

DRAWN BUTTER. Pure butterfat. Usually made by melting butter, discarding the frothy milk solids that rise to the top, and carefully ladling off the butterfat that floats on the water and whey. Also known as clarified butter.

EMULSIFY. To combine ingredients that normally separate, such as oil and vinegar, into a stable solution. Achieving this stability requires an emulsifying agent, such as egg yolks or mustard. Many salad dressings and vinaigrettes in this book call for this method.

FOLD. To gently combine ingredients (often with a rubber spatula) of different densities with a circular, bottom-to-top motion. Especially useful in pastry work, this technique is required for dishes such as chocolate mousse and soufflés.

GRATIN. Any dish topped with cheese or bread crumbs and baked until browned. Often used to refer to potato and pasta dishes.

MISE EN PLACE. In French, "things in their place." *Mise en place* encompasses everything you do ahead to prepare for the time when you're going to serve a meal, from boning a chicken to chopping parsley.

MOTHER SAUCE. In classic French cooking, this denotes a base sauce such as hollandaise or béchamel that can be made into numerous derivative, or small, sauces. This hierarchical method has been adapted to modern saucework, which utilizes a wider range of ingredients and often requires a lighter style. Many sauces in this book can be considered mother sauces, in that they are used as building blocks for many derivative sauces or variations. Sometimes called leading sauces.

PARFAIT. In French, "perfect." In culinary usage, a layered dessert with ice cream, sauce, and whipped cream, served in a tall glass; or a frozen custard.

PULSE. Used in this book to refer to a method of chopping or grinding ingredients in a food processor with an "on-off, on-off" action. Also commonly used to describe a number of dried legumes, including lentils, beans, and peas.

REDUCE; REDUCTION. To boil a liquid until it is reduced in volume. Reduction is the product of reducing a liquid, as in **Balsamic vinegar reduction**.

ROULADE. A "pinwheel" type of rolled preparation, such as sponge cake rolled around a filling; can also mean sliced meat, fish, or poultry rolled around a stuffing.

SEAR. To brown using high heat, usually in oil. Frequently done to prepare meat, poultry, or fish for another cooking method such as braising, roasting, or stewing. The caramelization thus produced is an important flavor component of many dishes.

SHOCK. A technique of instantly halting the cooking of an ingredient (when blanching, for example), usually by plunging into ice water. Sometimes called refreshing.

SHIMMER; SHIMMERS. When oil is hot enough for sautéing, it appears to shimmer in the pan and food added to it will sizzle. How quickly the oil will shimmer depends on the pan size, the amount of heat applied, and the amount of oil.

SLURRY. A combination of starch (such as cornstarch, potato, or tapioca) and cold liquid used to thicken soups, sauces, dressings, and custards.

SWEAT. To cook foods (usually savory vegetables such as onions and garlic) over low heat with a fat such as oil or butter, without browning, to soften food and release flavors.

TEMPER; TEMPERING. A method of raising temperature gradually in foods, to prevent curdling or lumping. Often achieved by adding hot liquid slowly to an ingredient such as egg yolks, when making a custard, for example.

Acknowledgments

Like a great journey, working on this book has been at turns challenging, exhausting, and incredibly rewarding. I've learned much—about myself, this magical area of Sonoma and the people who live here, the process of writing recipes, and the complexities involved in the evolution of ideas into print.

I need to thank many people:

First, the fantastic staff I've had the honor and pleasure to work with at the Ranch over the years: Maria, Graciela, Pen Leng, Patricia, Sylvia, and many more. I couldn't do it without you. You're the best!

Roberta Maran, for her sweet nature and enthusiasm from the beginning.

Robert Herzog, for his creative early layout work, photography, and generous contribution to the book.

Margaret Chapman, for understanding my creative needs, keeping accurate records, and for being the rock we all rely on.

Wendy Follen, for her love, humor, support, and many good suggestions.

Jill Hunting, for her meticulous editing skill, help in finding my voice and building a creative team, and wisdom and advice on all aspects of the self-publishing process, and my career as well.

Antonia Allegra, for her skillful coaching, encouragement, guidance, and unparalleled networking skills.

Steve Graydon, for his excellent graphic design work, and for keeping it fun.

Sandra Day, for proofing recipes, creating the index, and making many good suggestions.

The vendors of the Sonoma farmers market, for their hard work, good humor, and fine food from the good earth.

Sandy Shepard, for her lightning-fast legal advice.

The Westerbeke family, for creating the place that inspired this book and for their fun, outgoing natures.

Everyone owes a debt to those that have gone before: my thanks to Carol Bojarsky, for her original Westerbeke Ranch cookbook, *A Plate of Grace*, and all the thought and work that went into it. The stories therein still ring true.

Isa Jacoby, another longtime Ranch chef, for her help during busy times and her adventurous cuisine.

Rich Tashman, for originally inviting me to work at the ranch.

I thank you all and hope to enjoy many more years working, learning, and dancing through life with you.

Indexes

Index by Degree of Difficulty

Simple:

Moderate:

Challenging:

Index by Recipe Name and Ingredient

Order Form

Celebrating the Seasons at Westerbeke Ranch

Order online: go to **www.hppress.com**. Quantity discounts are available.

Order by phone: **800-325-3120, ext 6312 or ext 6310.**

Order by fax: **707-547-4562.**

Or fill out and clip form below, enclose check for total amount, and mail form and check to:

Global DocuGraphiX, Attn: Cookbook Order, PO Box 7789, Santa Rosa, CA 95407

Orders will be shipped within 48 hours.

- -

Please print

Name _____

Mailing Address _____

City _____ State _____ Zip _____

Daytime Phone (_____) _____ E-mail _____

I understand that my book(s) will be mailed to the address above.

☐ Enclosed is my check, payable to **Global DocuGraphiX.**

☐ Bill my credit card: ☐ **Mastercard** ☐ **Visa** ☐ **AMEX** ☐ **Discover**

_____   _____
Card Number   Expiration Date

_____
Signature

Quantity _____ x $19.95 =	$	
California residents, add 7.5% sales tax	$	
Plus shipping and handling*	$	
TOTAL	$	

Check payable to:
Global DocuGraphiX

Mail to:
Global DocuGraphiX
Attn: Cookbook Order
PO Box 7789
Santa Rosa, CA 95407

*1 book = $5.00. 2, 3 or 4 books = $6.00. More than 4, call 800-325-3120, ext 6312 or ext 6310. FedEx shipping prices listed for residential addresses. Business addresses, subtract $1.00.

- -

Thank you for your order!

Order Form

Celebrating the Seasons at Westerbeke Ranch

Order online: go to **www.hppress.com**. Quantity discounts are available.

Order by phone: **800-325-3120, ext 6312 or ext 6310.**

Order by fax: **707-547-4562.**

Or fill out and clip form below, enclose check for total amount, and mail form and check to:

Global DocuGraphiX, Attn: Cookbook Order, PO Box 7789, Santa Rosa, CA 95407

Orders will be shipped within 48 hours.

- -

Please print

Name _____

Mailing Address _____

City _____ **State** _____ **Zip** _____

Daytime Phone (_____) _____ **E-mail** _____

I understand that my book(s) will be mailed to the address above.

☐ Enclosed is my check, payable to **Global DocuGraphiX.**

☐ Bill my credit card: ☐ **Mastercard**   ☐ **Visa**   ☐ **AMEX**   ☐ **Discover**

_____

Card Number   **Expiration Date**

_____

Signature

Quantity _____ **x $19.95 =**	**$**	
California residents, add 7.5% sales tax	**$**	
Plus shipping and handling*	**$**	
TOTAL	**$**	

Check payable to:
Global DocuGraphiX

Mail to:
Global DocuGraphiX
Attn: Cookbook Order
PO Box 7789
Santa Rosa, CA 95407

*1 book = $5.00. 2, 3 or 4 books = $6.00. More than 4, call 800-325-3120, ext 6312 or ext 6310. FedEx shipping prices listed for residential addresses. Business addresses, subtract $1.00.

- -

Thank you for your order!